Love Intertwined

Behold Jesus Christ & His Beloved Disciples

Deborah Esther Nyamekye

©March 2016 Light of the World-John8.12 Publishing

All rights reserved.

ISBN 978-0-9931738-5-1

CONTENTS

Preface

Chapter 1	The Testimonies about Jesus Christ	1
Chapters 2 & 3	Jesus' Self-Description: A revelation of his Deity - The I Am Introduction: The "I Am" sayings of Jesus	14
Chapter 2	Seven "I Am" sayings of Jesus	19
Chapter 3	The eighth "I Am" saying: "I Am the True Vine"	38
Chapter 4	Jesus Christ, the All-Seeing and All-Knowing God and Prophet	53
Chapter 5	Jesus' authority, mission and preparation for His Crucifixion Part 1 Jesus' authority and expressions of his nature that reveal his mission Part 2 Jesus' discussions with his disciples close to the time of his crucifixion	69
Chapter 6	True disciples of Jesus Christ are legitimate children of God Part 1 The legitimate children of God in a New Covenant context Part 2 The chosen children of God and their ultimate destination	94
Chapter 7	What's in a Title? Descriptions of the mission of Jesus' disciples	119
Chapter 8	Jesus and his enemies, the unbelieving Jews Part 1 Jesus defies his enemies Part 2 The unbelieving Jews and religious leaders: lacked knowledge of the Son (Jesus), so could not know the Father	134
Chapter 9	The Bond of Love I – Jesus Christ and his female supporters	149
Chapter 10	The Bond of Love II–Jesus Christ, God the Father & the disciples	161

PREFACE

LOVE INTERTWINED: Behold Jesus Christ & His Beloved Disciples

When I began writing this book focusing mainly on the Gospel of John, but making reference to scriptures from other biblical books where required, I gradually acquired the full understanding of the type of book I was to write; a simple, concise and yet accurate insight into Scripture as revealed to me by the Holy Spirit. I felt inclined to focus on the Deity of Jesus Christ and his relationship with Father God, people in general and his disciples in particular. What is clear about this book is that it emphasises the

-centrality of Christ Jesus in the Christian faith and his Deity, as well as
-importance of a disciple of Jesus Christ cultivating an intimate relationship with God the Father through Jesus Christ.

I have felt inclined to call this book a Bible Study, Meditation and Devotional Manual because it can be used in any of these three ways; as an aid to reading, studying or meditating on Scripture. I have also included at the end of most of the chapters either a teaching, some counsel or words of encouragement.

Love Intertwined is a book that is easy to read and understand. Packed with scriptural references, it does not disappoint and is without a doubt beneficial to new and mature believers in Jesus Christ or anyone searching for the meaning of life.

May God richly bless you,

Deborah Esther Nyamekye
Ready Writer's Prophetic Scribe Ministry
A Subsidiary of Bear-witness Forerunner Ministries Int.

CHAPTER 1

THE TESTIMONIES ABOUT JESUS CHRIST

Introduction

What does it mean to testify? To testify is to bear witness by expressing or declaring a strong belief in something before
1. a formal deliberating body as in the case of a grand jury in court or
2. one or more people in a formal or informal assembly such as a church, a home or cell group of Christians. In this case the declaration of faith is in Jesus Christ or how faith in him has changed one's life.

When one testifies, one is giving a testimony which is a formal statement or evidence, written or spoken that supports or proves a fact. In court, such a formal statement (testimony) is given under oath to affirm that it is true. When a Christian testifies about their faith or their experiences of God, they are doing so based on the fact that they are "under oath" in terms of their covenant relationship with God. They are therefore presenting the facts as they know them to be true based on their relationship with God and His Word.

The Most High God, Abba Father also testified of who Jesus was, his coming to earth as well as his purpose or mission through prophets in Old Testament times.

1. The Apostle John testified in writing about Jesus Christ (John 1:1-18).

Jesus Christ is the Word who was in the beginning with God and is God. Jesus is the creator and as the Son of God on earth, he became the Saviour

- of the world. Through him all things were made; the world was made by him.
- He, the Word (of God) became flesh and came to dwell in the world so that mankind
  saw his Glory which is the Glory of God, the one and only God.
- He is one who came from Father full of His grace and truth.
- In him was life and that life was the true light in the life of every man.

"For this is how God loved the world: He gave his one and only Son, so that everyone who believes in him will not perish but have eternal life." (John 3:16 NLT).

2. The testimonies about Jesus; before, after his conception and directly after his birth.

i. The angel is sent by God to Mary and tells her that she is chosen by God to give birth to him. While doing so, the angel mentions the name of her child (Jesus) and testifies about him.

"In the sixth month of Elizabeth's pregnancy, God sent the angel Gabriel to Nazareth, a village in Galilee, 27 to a virgin named Mary. She was engaged to be married to a man named Joseph, a descendant of King David. 28 Gabriel appeared to her and said, "Greetings, favored woman! The Lord is with you!" 29 Confused and disturbed, Mary tried to think what the angel could mean. 30 "Don't be afraid, Mary," the angel told her, "for you have found favor with God! 31 You will conceive and give birth to a son, and you will name him Jesus. 32 He will be very great and will be called the Son of the Most High. The Lord God will give him the throne of his ancestor David.33 And he will reign over Israel forever; his Kingdom will never end!"
34 Mary asked the angel, "But how can this happen? I am a virgin."35 The angel replied, "The Holy Spirit will come upon you, and the power of the Most High will overshadow you. So the baby to be born will be holy, and he will be called the Son of God. 36 What's more, your relative Elizabeth has become pregnant in her old age! People used to say she was barren, but she has conceived a son and is now in her sixth month.37 For the word of God will never fail."38 Mary responded, "I am the

Lord's servant. May everything you have said about me come true." And then the angel left her." (Luke 1:26-38 NLT).

ii. Elizabeth, Mary's cousin and her unborn child in this manner testified of who Jesus was: Elizabeth was given utterance by the Holy Spirit that Mary is blessed by God after the baby in her womb leapt at the sound of Mary's greeting.

"A few days later Mary hurried to the hill country of Judea, to the town40 where Zechariah lived. She entered the house and greeted Elizabeth.41 At the sound of Mary's greeting, Elizabeth's child leaped within her, and Elizabeth was filled with the Holy Spirit.
42 Elizabeth gave a glad cry and exclaimed to Mary, "God has blessed you above all women, and your child is blessed. 43 Why am I so honored, that the mother of my Lord should visit me? 44 When I heard your greeting, the baby in my womb jumped for joy. 45 You are blessed because you believed that the Lord would do what he said." (Luke 1:39-45 NLT).

Elizabeth was as Mary, an intercessory vessel through whom the prophetic will of God (prophesied by Old Testament prophets) would be made manifest. Elizabeth was chosen to give birth to a child of promise who was prophesied to be a forerunner to Jesus (Luke 1:12-17/ John 1:19-27/ Isaiah 40:3-5). It was therefore not surprising that Elizabeth's child who was named John kicked in her womb when she heard Mary's greeting.

Mary was inspired to sing the following song of immense gratitude to God for choosing her among women, especially as she was a woman of low status.

> "Oh, how my soul praises the Lord.
> 47   How my spirit rejoices in God my Savior!
> 48 For he took notice of his lowly servant girl,
>   and from now on all generations will call me blessed.
> 49 For the Mighty One is holy,
>   and he has done great things for me.
> 50 He shows mercy from generation to generation
>   to all who fear him.
> 51 His mighty arm has done tremendous things!
>   He has scattered the proud and haughty ones.

52 He has brought down princes from their thrones
   and exalted the humble.
53 He has filled the hungry with good things
   and sent the rich away with empty hands.
54 He has helped his servant Israel
   and remembered to be merciful.
55 For he made this promise to our ancestors,
   to Abraham and his children forever."
56 Mary stayed with Elizabeth about three months
and then went back to her own home. (Luke 1:46-56 NLT).

The Shepherds testified to Mary and everyone about what the angels told them concerning Jesus after they saw the evidence themselves.

"That night there were shepherds staying in the fields nearby, guarding their flocks of sheep. 9 Suddenly, an angel of the Lord appeared among them, and the radiance of the Lord's glory surrounded them. They were terrified, 10 but the angel reassured them. "Don't be afraid!" he said. "I bring you good news that will bring great joy to all people.11 The Savior—yes, the Messiah, the Lord—has been born today in Bethlehem, the city of David! 12 And you will recognize him by this sign: You will find a baby wrapped snugly in strips of cloth, lying in a manger."13 Suddenly, the angel was joined by a vast host of others—the armies of heaven—praising God and saying,14 "Glory to God in highest heaven, and peace on earth to those with whom God is pleased." 15 When the angels had returned to heaven, the shepherds said to each other, "Let's go to Bethlehem! Let's see this thing that has happened, which the Lord has told us about."
16 They hurried to the village and found Mary and Joseph. And there was the baby, lying in the manger. 17 After seeing him, the shepherds told everyone what had happened and what the angel had said to them about this child. 18 All who heard the shepherds' story were astonished, 19 but Mary kept all these things in her heart and thought about them often. 20 The shepherds went back to their flocks, glorifying and praising God for all they had heard and seen. It was just as the angel had told them." (Luke 2:8-20 NLT).

iii. The act of following the star by wise men from the east was a testimony to the fact that Jesus Christ the Messiah had been born. They received a clear revelation from God about who the

star would lead them to, "The King of the Jews" (Jesus Christ) and they obeyed.

"Jesus was born in Bethlehem in Judea, during the reign of King Herod. About that time some wise men from eastern lands arrived in Jerusalem, asking, 2 "Where is the new born king of the Jews? We saw his star as it rose, and we have come to worship him."
3 King Herod was deeply disturbed when he heard this, as was everyone in Jerusalem. 4 He called a meeting of the leading priests and teachers of religious law and asked, "Where is the Messiah supposed to be born?"
5 "In Bethlehem in Judea," they said, "for this is what the prophet wrote:
6 'And you, O Bethlehem in the land of Judah,
   are not least among the ruling cities of Judah,
for a ruler will come from you
   who will be the shepherd for my people Israel."
7 Then Herod called for a private meeting with the wise men, and he learned from them the time when the star first appeared. 8 Then he told them, "Go to Bethlehem and search carefully for the child. And when you find him, come back and tell me so that I can go and worship him, too!"
9 After this interview the wise men went their way. And the star they had seen in the east guided them to Bethlehem. It went ahead of them and stopped over the place where the child was. 10 When they saw the star, they were filled with joy! 11 They entered the house and saw the child with his mother, Mary, and they bowed down and worshiped him. Then they opened their treasure chests and gave him gifts of gold, frankincense, and myrrh.
12 When it was time to leave, they returned to their own country by another route, for God had warned them in a dream not to return to Herod." (Matthew 2:1-12 NLT).
The testimonies of two elderly Jewish prophetic intercessors in the temple who were
waiting for the birth of Jesus Christ.

When Mary and Joseph took Jesus to the temple they met elderly Jews, Anna and Simeon. They had received supernatural revelation of Jesus Christ as the promised Messiah to come and believed God. Upon seeing Jesus, they glorified God and testified about what God had said to them about him.

A. SIMEON:

"At that time there was a man in Jerusalem named Simeon. He was righteous and devout and was eagerly waiting for the Messiah to come and rescue Israel. The Holy Spirit was upon him 26 and had revealed to him that he would not die until he had seen the Lord's Messiah. 27 That day the Spirit led him to the Temple. So when Mary and Joseph came to present the baby Jesus to the Lord as the law required, 28 Simeon was there. He took the child in his arms and praised God, saying,

29 "Sovereign Lord, now let your servant die in peace,
as you have promised.
30 I have seen your salvation,
31 which you have prepared for all people.
32 He is a light to reveal God to the nations,
   and he is the glory of your people Israel!"
33 Jesus' parents were amazed at what was being said about him. 34 Then Simeon blessed them, and he said to Mary, the baby's mother, "This child is destined to cause many in Israel to fall, but he will be a joy to many others. He has been sent as a sign from God, but many will oppose him. 35 As a result, the deepest thoughts of many hearts will be revealed. And a sword will pierce your very soul." (Luke 2:25-35 NLT).

B. ANNA:

"Anna, a prophet, was also there in the Temple. She was the daughter of Phanuel from the tribe of Asher, and she was very old. Her husband died when they had been married only seven years. 37 Then she lived as a widow to the age of eighty-four. She never left the Temple but stayed there day and night, worshiping God with fasting and prayer.38 She came along just as Simeon was talking with Mary and Joseph, and she began praising God. She talked about the child to everyone who had been waiting expectantly for God to rescue Jerusalem."(Luke 2:36-38 NLT).

As Mary, Simeon and Anna accepted their calling and believed that God would keep His promise to them. Both are 24/7 prophetic intercessors, birthers or spiritual mothers who as Mary did in the natural sense with Jesus, carried the promise of God (that they would see the Messiah) to full term or until it was made manifest. Anna was also an evangelist on behalf of Jesus, well before Jesus

was born and therefore well before the great commission of Jesus to his disciples prior to his ascension:
"Jesus came and told his disciples, "I have been given all authority in heaven and on earth. 19 Therefore, go and make disciples of all the nations,[a] baptizing them in the name of the Father and the Son and the Holy Spirit.20 Teach these new disciples to obey all the commands I have given you. And be sure of this: I am with you always, even to the end of the age." (Matthew 18:18-20 NLT).

iv. Mary testified of who Jesus was when she told wedding hosts to do whatever he tells them. Her words set in motion Jesus' first miracle which was a testimony of who he was as a miracle worker and one who had the glory of God. This resulted in his disciples believing in him (John 2:11).

"The next day there was a wedding celebration in the village of Cana in Galilee. Jesus' mother was there, 2 and Jesus and his disciples were also invited to the celebration. 3 The wine supply ran out during the festivities, so Jesus' mother told him, "They have no more wine." 4 "Dear woman, that's not our problem," Jesus replied. "My time has not yet come." 5 But his mother told the servants, "Do whatever he tells you." 6 Standing nearby were six stone water jars, used for Jewish ceremonial washing. Each could hold twenty to thirty gallons.7 Jesus told the servants, "Fill the jars with water." When the jars had been filled, 8 he said, "Now dip some out, and take it to the master of ceremonies." So the servants followed his instructions.9 When the master of ceremonies tasted the water that was now wine, not knowing where it had come from (though, of course, the servants knew), he called the bridegroom over.10 "A host always serves the best wine first," he said. "Then, when everyone has had a lot to drink, he brings out the less expensive wine. But you have kept the best until now!"11 This miraculous sign at Cana in Galilee was the first time Jesus revealed his glory. And his disciples believed in him." (John 2: 1-11 NTL).

Jesus' reply to his mother Mary when she told him that there was no more wine at the wedding 4 "Dear woman, that's not our problem,.. My time has not yet come." (John 2:4 NLT), was not said in expectation of a reply from her. Jesus was saying indirectly that his time for his blood to be shed through crucifixion had not yet come. He was likening his blood to the Passover wine which he would later refer to as the cup of the new covenant as he had Passover supper with his disciples on the same night he was betrayed (Luke 22:20/1 Corinthians 11:23).

Just prior to the wedding in Cana, Jesus had been empowered for ministry through baptism in water and the Holy Spirit (John 1:29-34). When Mary told Jesus "They're out of wine" and then told the servants to do whatever Jesus tells them to do, she was being used by God to set the stage for this first miracle in his public ministry. Mary was not only chosen to give birth to Jesus, the Saviour of the world but also to testify of who he was as a confirmation of what she knew to be true (see points i-v). She was available to God at every opportunity to testify of her son's purpose and being God's instrument to set the stage for his first miracle was one of them. This miracle Mary was used by God to set in motion, would in itself testify of who Jesus was as the Son of God because through him the power of God would be demonstrated (John 2:11).

3. John the Baptist testified of Jesus Christ.

Even as a foetus in his mother's womb, John the Baptist recognised the voice of the woman chosen to be Jesus' mother just after Jesus was conceived by the Holy Spirit.
As an adult, John the Baptist preached that he came to prepare the way for Jesus by baptizing with water so that Jesus who will baptise with the Holy Spirit might be revealed to Israel.

When asked who he was, "John replied in the words of the prophet Isaiah: "I am a voice shouting in the wilderness, 'Clear the way for the Lord's coming!'" (John 1:23 NLT).

John said the following about Jesus "I did not recognize him as the Messiah, but I have been baptizing with water so that he might be revealed to Israel. I saw the Holy Spirit descending like a dove from heaven and resting upon him. 33 I didn't know he was the one, but when God sent me to baptize with water, he told me, 'The one on whom you see the Spirit descend and rest is the one who will baptize with the Holy Spirit.' 34 I saw this happen to Jesus, so I testify that he is the Chosen One of God." (John 1: 31-34 NLT).

The Holy Spirit's descent on Jesus Christ according to the Word of God enabled John the Baptist to know and therefore testify of Jesus as the Messiah or "The Chosen one of God", Israel had been waiting for.

John the Baptist also testified of what God told him about Jesus as follows (John 1:15-18 NLT):

- Although born on earth after John the Baptist, Jesus is greater than him because he existed long before him.

- Jesus is God and the only one capable of revealing God to mankind who have never seen God.

- Jesus is the Saviour, the Lamb of God that takes away the sins of the World (John 1:29 NLT).

- The Spirit filled Son of God who will baptise with the Holy Spirit (John 1:32-34 NLT).

4. Jesus Christ's disciples testified of him.

- Andrew was one of two disciples of John the Baptist who left him and became disciples of Jesus:
  "Andrew went to find his brother, Simon, and told him, "We have found the Messiah" (which means "Christ").42 Then Andrew brought Simon to meet Jesus. Looking intently at Simon, Jesus said, "Your name is Simon, son of John—but you will be called Cephas" (which means "Peter")." (John 1:41-42 NLT).

- The Apostle Matthew recounts how Christ Jesus asked his disciples who they thought he was, "Simon Peter answered,

"You are the Messiah, the Son of the living God." (Matthew 16:16 NLT).

- "John testified about him when he shouted to the crowds, "This is the one I was talking about when I said, 'Someone is coming after me who is far greater than I am, for he existed long before me.'"16 From his abundance we have all received one gracious blessing after another. 17 For the law was given through Moses, but God's unfailing love and faithfulness came through Jesus Christ. 18 No one has ever seen God. But the unique One, who is himself God, is near to the Father's heart. He has revealed God to us." (John 1:15-18 NLT).

- Philip was called as a disciple by Jesus and "Philip went to look for Nathanael and told him, "We have found the very person Moses and the prophets wrote about! His name is Jesus, the son of Joseph from Nazareth. "Nazareth!" exclaimed Nathanael. "Can anything good come from Nazareth?" "Come and see for yourself," Philip replied. (John 1:45-46 NLT).

- After listening to Jesus (John 1:47-48) Nathanael was convinced of who Jesus was and said "Rabbi, you are the Son of God—the King of Israel!" (John 1:49 NLT).

5. Nicodemus, a Pharisee testified that Jesus was sent by God to teach Israel.

"There was a man named Nicodemus, a Jewish religious leader who was a Pharisee. ² After dark one evening, he came to speak with Jesus. "Rabbi," he said, "we all know that God has sent you to teach us. Your miraculous signs are evidence that God is with you." (John 3:1-2 NLT)

6. God testified openly that Jesus is His dearly loved Son who brings him great joy.

"After his baptism, as Jesus came up out of the water, the heavens were opened and he saw the Spirit of God descending like a dove and settling on him. [17] And a voice from heaven said, "This is my dearly loved Son, who brings me great joy." (Matthew 3:16-17NLT).

7. The Holy Spirit testified of Jesus Christ.

- God revealed to John the Baptist that the Holy Spirit was upon Jesus, and this confirmed to him who Jesus was otherwise he would not have recognized Jesus;

  "Then John testified, "I saw the Holy Spirit descending like a dove from heaven and resting upon him. 33 I didn't know he was the one, but when God sent me to baptize with water, he told me, 'The one on whom you see the Spirit descend and rest is the one who will baptize with the Holy Spirit.' 34 I saw this happen to Jesus, so I testify that he is the Chosen One of God." (John 1:32-34 NLT).

- The Holy Spirit was sent by God to Jesus' disciples at the time and continues to be sent to those who become Jesus' disciples because Jesus prayed for this to happen prior to his death so that as our guide, teacher, helper and comforter he would be as a parent ensuring we do not feel like orphans who are abandoned or rejected. The nature of The Holy Spirit is the nature of Jesus Christ.

  For more on the Holy Spirit, see Chapters 6, point IIA & end of chapter section "Teaching ~ Encouragement"

Encouragement

You are the Light of the World, a Living Testimony!

"Jesus spoke to the people once more and said, "I am the Light of the World. If you follow me, you won't have to walk in darkness, because you will have the light that leads to life." (John 8:12 NLT).

"The Son radiates God's own glory and expresses the very character of God, and he sustains everything by the mighty power of his command. When he had cleansed us from our sins, he sat down in the place of honour at the right hand of the majestic God in heaven." (Hebrews 1:3 NLT).

As a Christian, having accepted Jesus Christ as your Lord and Saviour, you are the Light of the World in Christ-likeness and your calling is not only to survive and overcome the kingdom of darkness but to testify of who Christ is, emitting his radiance wherever you go and in whatever you do, to the glory of God. Your very existence and lifestyle as a true child of God is a living testimony that God's power through Christ is being made manifest in the world, transforming the atmosphere and individual lives. The darkness speaks of Satan's world of evil and wicked deeds.
This is a promise to you as it is to the Israelites:

> "Arise, Jerusalem! Let your light shine for all to see.
> "For the glory of the LORD rises to shine on you.
> 2 Darkness as black as night covers all the nations of the earth,
> but the glory of the LORD rises and appears over you.
> 3 All nations will come to your light; mighty kings will come to
> see your radiance."(Isaiah 60:1-3 NLT).

Imagine the magnitude of the radiance of God emitted through a congregation of true believers, Christ's "Light bearers"!

God wants to bring to your remembrance the following uplifting word spoken by Christ, so that you fulfil your destiny according to God's will:

Meditate on these encouraging words spoken by Christ to his disciples:

"You are the light of the world—like a city on a hilltop that cannot be hidden. 15 No one lights a lamp and then puts it under a basket. Instead, a lamp is placed on a stand, where it gives light to everyone in the house. 16 In the same way, let your good deeds shine out for all to see, so that everyone will praise your heavenly Father." (Matt.5:14-16 NLT).

CHAPTERS 2 & 3

JESUS' SELF-DESCRIPTION: A REVELATION OF HIS DEITY – THE I AM.

- INTRODUCTION – CHAPTERS 2 & 3
  THE "I AM" SAYINGS OF JESUS

- CHAPTER 2
  SEVEN "I AM" SAYINGS OF JESUS

- CHAPTER 3
  THE EIGHTH "I AM" SAYING: "I AM THE TRUE VINE"

INTRODUCTION

THE "I AM" SAYINGS OF JESUS

Jesus referred to himself in different ways, however these are eight distinct ways he referred to himself which have I AM in the phrase:

1. I am the Bread of Life.
"Jesus replied, "I am the bread of life. Whoever comes to me will never be hungry again. Whoever believes in me will never be thirsty." (John 6:35 NLT)

2. I am the Light of the World.
"Jesus spoke to the people once more and said, "I am the light of the world. If you follow me, you won't have to walk in darkness, because you will have the light that leads to life." (John 8:12 NLT)

3. I am the Gate (Door).
"⁹ Yes, I am the gate. Those who come in through me will be saved. They will come and go freely and will find good pastures." (John 10:9 NLT)

4. I am the Good Shepherd.
"I am the good shepherd. The good shepherd sacrifices his life for the sheep." (John 10:11 NLT)

5. I am the Resurrection and The Life.
"I am the resurrection and the life. Anyone who believes in me will live, even after dying. ²⁶ Everyone who lives in me and believes in me will never ever die. Do you believe this, Martha?" (John 11:25-26 NLT)

6. I am the Way, the Truth and the Life.
"Jesus told him, "I am the way, the truth, and the life. No one can come to the Father except through me." (John 14:6 NLT)

7. Before Abraham was I Am.
"Jesus answered, "I tell you the truth, before Abraham was even born, I AM!" (John 8:58 NLT)

8. I am the Vine.
"Yes, I am the vine; you are the branches. Those who remain in me, and I in them, will produce much fruit. For apart from me you can do nothing." (John 15:5NLT).

When Jesus referred to himself in the first seven different ways listed above, he was affirming

1. The different expressions of his deity or nature as the Most High God.
   It is only when he said (point 7) "before Abraham was, I AM (John 8:58) that he stated plainly that he is God. Jesus was explaining through referring to himself in the first seven different ways listed above that he is life-giving and therefore transforming in nature as God is and this is

because he is actually God therefore existing even before Abraham.

2. He is a prophet who came to

- be the mouthpiece of the Father (Most High God).
  Jesus said
  "The words I speak are not my own..." (John 14:10 NLT)
  "I don't speak on my own authority. The Father who sent me has commanded me what to say and how to say it." (John 12:49 NLT)

- do His works;
  Jesus was anointed by the Father to heal the sick, broken hearted, oppressed, to cast out demons, rebuild ruined lives and teach about the Kingdom.

  "...Jesus explained, "I tell you the truth, the Son can do nothing by himself. He does only what he sees the Father doing. Whatever the Father does, the Son also does." (John 5:19 NLT)

  Jesus quoted from Isaiah 61:1-2 in reference to himself as follows
  "The Spirit of the LORD is upon me, for he has anointed me to bring Good News to the poor. He has sent me to proclaim that captives will be released, that the blind will see, that the oppressed will be set free and that the time of the Lord's favor has come." He rolled up the scroll, handed it back to the attendant, and sat down. All eyes in the synagogue looked at him intently. (Luke 4:18-10NLT).

  "And you know that God anointed Jesus of Nazareth with the Holy Spirit and with power. Then Jesus went around doing good and healing all who were oppressed by the devil, for God was with him." (Act 10:38NLT).

3. He loves mankind and is relational: This is why each of the first 7 expressions of his deity (Life-giving because he came to redeem or transform lives) are as such because they are for the purpose of explaining who he is to mankind; for instance Life-giver, Saviour, Carer and Protector.

   The Apostle John states in 1 John 4:8 that "God is Love". The Most High God never stopped loving His creation even though starting with Adam and Eve, they constantly sinned against him and so chose to disobey him. God planned before the foundations of the world that the descendants of Adam and Eve would be offered a means through which they can be restored into covenant with Him. God decided that He would come himself in the person of Jesus Christ to dwell among men and be their redeemer. This is why the Apostle Paul said
   "For God was in Christ, reconciling the world to himself, no longer counting people's sins against them. And he gave us this wonderful message of reconciliation." (2 Corinthians 5:19NLT).

   Reconciliation of the world back to God starts with reconciliation of man. Jesus Christ (God as man) came to do so through his death, burial and resurrection so that anyone who confesses and believes in their heart that he is Lord and Saviour will not perish but have eternal life (Romans 10:9-10). During his ministry, he taught about how his disciples could live lives as a truly reconciled people with God and in so doing who also through Christ have the ministry of reconciliation towards others.

In summary, it is evident that Jesus' descriptions of himself in these eight ways explain his

1. Deity or nature as God,
2. His relationship with God, the Father who sent him and
3. His relationship with his disciples:

-The type of people who qualify as his true disciples.
-How he would like his disciples to relate to him.

Chapter 2 discusses the first seven listed "I AM" sayings of Jesus (above) and Chapter 3 discusses the eighth listed, namely "I am the Vine".

CHAPTER 2

SEVEN "I AM" SAYINGS OF JESUS

I.   **"I am the Way, the Truth, and the Life"
    incorporating:**

- "I am the Resurrection and Life"
- "I am the Light of the World"
- "Before Abraham was I AM"

John Chapter 14

"Don't let your hearts be troubled. Trust in God, and trust also in me. ² There is more than enough room in my Father's home. If this were not so, would I have told you that I am going to prepare a place for you? ³ When everything is ready, I will come and get you, so that you will always be with me where I am. ⁴ And you know the way to where I am going."
⁵ "No, we don't know, Lord," Thomas said. "We have no idea where you are going, so how can we know the way?" ⁶ Jesus told him, "I am the way, the truth, and the life. No one can come to the Father except through me.

"If you had really known me, you would know who my Father is. From now on, you do know him and have seen him!" ⁸ Philip said, "Lord, show us the Father, and we will be satisfied."
⁹ Jesus replied, "Have I been with you all this time, Philip, and yet you still don't know who I am? Anyone who has seen me has seen the Father! So why are you asking me to show him to you? ¹⁰ Don't you believe that I am in the Father and the Father is in me? The words I speak are not my own, but my Father who lives in me does his work through me. ¹¹ Just believe that I am in the Father and the Father is in me. Or at least believe because of the work you have seen me do.
¹² "I tell you the truth, anyone who believes in me will do the same works I have done, and even greater works, because I am going to be with the

Father. ¹³ You can ask for anything in my name, and I will do it, so that the Son can bring glory to the Father. ¹⁴ Yes, ask me for anything in my name, and I will do it!

¹⁵ "If you love me, obey my commandments. ¹⁶ And I will ask the Father, and he will give you another Advocate, who will never leave you. ¹⁷ He is the Holy Spirit, who leads into all truth. The world cannot receive him, because it isn't looking for him and doesn't recognize him. But you know him, because he lives with you now and later will be in you. ¹⁸ No, I will not abandon you as orphans—I will come to you. ¹⁹ Soon the world will no longer see me, but you will see me. Since I live, you also will live. ²⁰ When I am raised to life again, you will know that I am in my Father, and you are in me, and I am in you. ²¹ Those who accept my commandments and obey them are the ones who love me. And because they love me, my Father will love them. And I will love them and reveal myself to each of them."

²² Judas (not Judas Iscariot, but the other disciple with that name) said to him, "Lord, why are you going to reveal yourself only to us and not to the world at large?"
²³ Jesus replied, "All who love me will do what I say. My Father will love them, and we will come and make our home with each of them. ²⁴ Anyone who doesn't love me will not obey me. And remember, my words are not my own. What I am telling you is from the Father who sent me. ²⁵ I am telling you these things now while I am still with you. ²⁶ But when the Father sends the Advocate as my representative—that is, the Holy Spirit—he will teach you everything and will remind you of everything I have told you.

²⁷ "I am leaving you with a gift—peace of mind and heart. And the peace I give is a gift the world cannot give. So don't be troubled or afraid. ²⁸ Remember what I told you: I am going away, but I will come back to you again. If you really loved me, you would be happy that I am going to the Father, who is greater than I am. ²⁹ I have told you these things before they happen so that when they do happen, you will believe. ³⁰ "I don't have much more time to talk to you, because the ruler of this world approaches. He has no power over me, ³¹ but I will do what the Father requires of me, so that the world will know that I love the Father. Come, let's be going." (NLT)

A. Jesus Christ and God "The I AM" are one and the same.

Jesus said that he is "the Way, the Truth and the Life" and no one can come to God the Father except through him (John 14:6).

Summary:

Jesus is
- The Way: He is the only Way to Father, and therefore is The Way to the Father (God).
- The Truth: He is a revelation of Father's Truth and therefore he is as God, The Truth.
- The Life: A giver of abundant life and eternal life. He is life-giving as a redeemer and is therefore The Life of God.

Jesus as THE WAY means that as God in the flesh who came as a sacrificial lamb and as a priest to redeem mankind from a life of sin destined for hell and in His nature as God's Prophetic vessel through whom God communicates with mankind, he is the only means through whom mankind and God are reconciled. The Way for mankind to have access to God.

Jesus' nature as The Way encompasses his nature as
-The Truth of God and
-The Life of God.

A Discourse resulting in the conclusion that Jesus and the Father are one: Jesus Christ is God the Creator in flesh, who sent him through the nation of Israel.

a) God's Truth sets Jesus' disciples free from Satan's bondage and deception:

"And you will know the truth, and the truth will set you free."(John 8:32 NLT).

God's Truth is transforming and Life-giving. Therefore God's Truth is synonymous with God's Life that transforms.

Conclusion:
God's Truth and Life (both personified by Jesus, The Way) have the same meaning in the context of describing who God of our Lord Jesus Christ is, but expressed in different ways.

Point b, below affirms this:

   b) God is Spirit, He is also The Truth and The Life.

1.God is Spirit and He is also The Truth.

"But the time is coming—indeed it's here now—when true worshipers will worship the Father in spirit and in truth. The Father is looking for those who will worship him that way. 24 For God is Spirit, so those who worship him must worship in spirit and in truth." (John 4:23-24 NLT).

Truth in John 4:23-24 refers to God's (who is Spirit) Truth. Jesus, "The Truth" personifies God's "Truth" (John 14:6).

2. i. God is Spirit and He is also The Life.
Jesus said "The Spirit alone gives eternal life. Human effort accomplishes nothing. And the very words I have spoken to you are spirit and life." (John 6:63NLT).

"The Spirit" here refers to God who is Spirit and the giver of eternal life.

Therefore Eternal life or Life in John 6:63 refers to God's (who is Spirit) Life. Jesus "The Life" personifies God's "Life" (John 14:6).

ii. Jesus said the following

"I don't speak on my own authority. The Father who sent me has commanded me what to say and how to say it.⁵⁰ And I know his commands lead to eternal life; so I say whatever the Father tells me to say." (John 12:49-50 NLT).

"My message is not my own; it comes from God who sent me. (John 7:16NLT).

"Don't you believe that I am in the Father and the Father is in me? The words I speak are not my own, but my Father who lives in me does his work through me." (John 14:10NLT).

Conclusion of b) 2 i. and 2 ii.
In reference to John 6:63, we can conclude that Jesus is saying that his "Spirit and Life" words are an expression of the nature of their source, God the Father, because his words are from Him (John 12:49-50/7:16/14:10 see b) 2 ii.)

From John 6:63, Jesus' words are "Spirit" and "Life": Let's see how the "Spirit and Life" Words of Jesus are an expression of God's nature, which is also Jesus' nature:

1. God is "Spirit" and therefore "The Truth".
The words spoken by Jesus (John 6:63) are Spirit: This also refers to the Holy Spirit of God or the power of God.

The Holy Spirit is said to be the Spirit of Truth by Jesus. As the Holy Spirit is God's Spirit, he was in essence describing the nature of God as "The Truth".

Jesus was also pointing out that The Truth (God) exposes and overcomes satanic deception and sets captives of Satan free (John 8:32).

2. God is "Life" and therefore "The Truth"

The words spoken by Jesus (John 6:63) are Life: God through Christ as a redeemer is life-giving and therefore transforming hence "The Life".

The life giving and transforming nature of God bears witness to His nature as The Truth. This is because when one accepts Jesus as Lord and Saviour, the Life of God within testifies of God's true Word (His Truth) which is contrary to Satan's lies and has the power to deliver the believer in Jesus from their evil ways; satanic bondage and deception (John 8:32).

We can conclude that
God is Spirit and He is also
-The Life and
-The Truth
When we say God is Spirit, God is The Life and God is The Truth, we are expressing who God is in three different ways although we mean the same thing. Thus in describing God, all three: Spirit, The Life and The Truth are synonymous.

c) Point b)'s conclusion reminds us of who Jesus said he is according to John 14:6.

1. The Way, The Truth and the Life : meaning He is The Way (in the sense of the only Way) to the Father who is Spirit, The Truth and The Life.
Jesus is one with God who is Spirit:

The Apostle Paul called Jesus the Last Adam the Life giving Spirit (1 Corinth.15:45) he was saying that as the redeemer who came to deliver mankind from the generational sin of Adam and Eve (disobedience to God which brought about separation), he was doing so in his nature as God, the "Life giving Spirit". Jesus had spoken of God as "Spirit" and should be worshipped in Spirit and in Truth.

2.The Truth : He is in oneness with God who is the Truth.

3. The Life: He is in oneness with God who is The Life.
Jesus said "I am the Light of the World, he who comes to me will have the Light of Life" (John 8:12).

Here we see that Jesus equates His Light with Life or the Life of God. Hence his nature as Light is the same as his nature as The Life (God) because as one who exposes darkness (evil) and delivers people from the kingdom of darkness (Satan), he is manifesting as the "Last Adam, the Life-giving Spirit" (The Apostle Paul's description of Jesus in 1 Corinth. 15:45).

The affirmation derived from this whole section (a)-c)) is that Jesus is indeed God or one with God as He expressed in the following ways:

- "I and my Father are one" (John 10:30).
- "If you have seen me you have seen the Father" (John 14: 14:7,9)
- He spoke of oneness with Father & prayed for believers in him that they would also be one (John 17:21).
- Before Abraham was I AM. This is one of the I Am sayings of Jesus.

"BEFORE ABRAHAM WAS I AM" (John 8:58)
Jesus spoke of himself as one who existed before creation, meaning he is God.

God referred to himself as "I AM" in the Old Testament when he was speaking to Moses

[13] But Moses protested, "If I go to the people of Israel and tell them, 'The God of your ancestors has sent me to you,' they will ask me, 'What is his name?' Then what should I tell them?" [14] God replied to Moses, "I AM WHO I AM.Say this to the people of Israel:I AM has sent me to you." [15] God also said to Moses, "Say this to the people of Israel: Yahweh, the God of your ancestors—the God of Abraham, the God of Isaac, and the God of Jacob—has sent me to

you. This is my eternal name, my name to remember for all generations."(Exodus 3:13-14NLT)

Jesus also refers to himself as the "I AM" in John 8 when he was in conversation with the unbelieving religious leaders as follows.

⁵² The people said, "Now we know you are possessed by a demon. Even Abraham and the prophets died, but you say, 'Anyone who obeys my teaching will never die!' ⁵³ Are you greater than our father Abraham? He died, and so did the prophets. Who do you think you are?" ⁵⁴ Jesus answered, "If I want glory for myself, it doesn't count. But it is my Father who will glorify me. You say, 'He is our God,'
⁵⁵ but you don't even know him. I know him. If I said otherwise, I would be as great a liar as you! But I do know him and obey him. ⁵⁶ Your father Abraham rejoiced as he looked forward to my coming. He saw it and was glad."
⁵⁷ The people said, "You aren't even fifty years old. How can you say you have seen Abraham?"⁵⁸ Jesus answered, "I tell you the truth, before Abraham was even born, I AM!" ⁵⁹ At that point they picked up stones to throw at him. But Jesus was hidden from them and left the Temple. (John 8:52-59NLT)

OTHER AUTHORS OF BIBLICAL BOOKS ALSO EXPRESS THE DEITY OF JESUS CHRIST:

The above manner in which Jesus testifies of himself as God reminds us of other people's testimonies of Jesus which confirm that he is God and was sent by God (see Chapter 1). The Author of the biblical book of Hebrews and the Apostle Paul wrote about the Deity of Jesus Christ as follows:

1. **HEBREWS**

In Hebrews Chapter one, it is stated that God referred to Jesus as himself (Heb. 1:8) and also in another sentence as belonging to Him (Heb.1:9).

"8 But to the Son he says,
"Your throne, O God, endures forever and ever.
　You rule with a scepter of justice.
9 You love justice and hate evil.
　Therefore, O God, your God has anointed you,
　pouring out the oil of joy on you more than on anyone else."
(Heb.1:8-9 NLT)

Jesus' character and what he does is descriptive of God's character and what He does; Jesus' character as one who loves righteousness and hates sin or iniquity is descriptive of that of God. (Heb.1:9).

In Hebrews chapters 1 and 2, we read about the author of Hebrews' reference to Jesus as Creator and Saviour in a manner that brings to mind the names of God; Adonai (the Sovereign God of all) & El Elyon (The Most High God, Creator, Possessor of the whole universe):

The scriptures in Hebrews particularly Hebrews 1:3,10 and 2:10 resonate what is written in many biblical verses identifying Jesus as God, the Creator and Saviour who manifests His presence and glory as the Light of the world to overcome a dark evil world.

"He also says to the Son, "In the beginning, Lord, you laid the foundation of the earth and made the heavens with your hands."" (Hebrews 1:10 NLT)

"[2] And now in these final days, he has spoken to us through his Son. God promised everything to the Son as an inheritance, and through the Son he created the universe.[3] The Son radiates God's own glory and expresses the very character of God, and he sustains everything by the mighty power of his command. When he had cleansed us from our sins, he sat down in the place of honor at the right hand of the majestic God in heaven."(Hebrews 1:2-3 NLT).

"[10] God, for whom and through whom everything was made, chose to bring many children into glory. And it was only right that he should make Jesus, through his suffering, a perfect leader, fit to bring them into their salvation." (Heb.2:10 NLT).

2. CORINTHIANS

"[19] For God was in Christ, reconciling the world to himself, no longer counting people's sins against them. And he gave us this wonderful message of reconciliation." (2 Corinthians 5:19NLT).

3. COLOSSIANS

" Christ is the visible image of the invisible God.
  He existed before anything was created and is supreme over all creation,
[16] for through him God created everything
  in the heavenly realms and on earth.
He made the things we can see
  and the things we can't see—
such as thrones, kingdoms, rulers, and authorities in the unseen world.
  Everything was created through him and for him.
[17] He existed before anything else,
  and he holds all creation together.
[18] Christ is also the head of the church,
  which is his body.
He is the beginning,
  supreme over all who rise from the dead.[1]
  So he is first in everything.
[19] For God in all his fullness
  was pleased to live in Christ,
[20] and through him God reconciled
  everything to himself.
He made peace with everything in heaven and on earth
  by means of Christ's blood on the cross. (Col.1:15-20NLT)

"For in Christ lives all the fullness of God in a human body" (Col. 2:9NLT)

B. THE TYPE OF DISCIPLES JESUS SEEKS

Jesus' words in John 14 give profound insight into what he meant when he said "I am the Way, Truth and the Life" (John 14:6) in relation to himself as well as people who are his disciples or are considering becoming his disciples.

In this chapter (John 14) we gain the understanding that His desire is that those who are his disciples

1. Through knowing Jesus, they accept that they also know the Father and have seen him because as he said "I am in the Father and the Father is in me". A true disciple of Jesus must gain the revelation that Jesus and Father God are one (vs 7-11), Philip at the time had not gained that revelation as yet which is why he said ""Lord, show us the Father, and we will be satisfied."

2. Know that believing in Jesus as their Lord and Saviour inevitably endows them with the spiritual ability to do the works Jesus does and even greater works (vs 12)
   This means that as disciples of Jesus, the Father is in them as He is in Jesus for in addition to saying that he was in the Father and the Father is in him, Jesus also said that the words he spoke to them are not his own but his Fathers. In addition, it is His Father who lives in him who does His work through Jesus.

   Jesus' disciples in the church following his ascension to the Father are promised to do greater works than he did (vs 12), this is because of the promise of the Holy Spirit to those who are obedient to Jesus (vs 15). It is therefore noteworthy that a sign of being a disciple and therefore eligible for the guidance and infilling of the Holy Spirit is obedience to Jesus' commandments.

   Jesus said "If you love me, obey my commandments. 16 And I will ask the Father, and he will give you another Advocate, who will never leave you. 17 He is the Holy Spirit, who leads into all truth. The world cannot receive him, because it isn't looking for him and doesn't recognize him. But you know him, because he lives with you now and later will be in you. 18 No, I will not abandon you as orphans—I will come to you." (John 14:15-18 NLT).

The Holy Spirit came on the day of Pentecost (Acts 2:1-13) and has been with and within Jesus' disciples since so that it is as though Jesus never left them (vs 18-20). The Holy Spirit, the Spirit and power of God bears witness to Jesus (Rev 19:10/John 15, 26-27) and with the Spirit of believers (Romans 8:15) in Jesus that they are children of God.

A believer in Jesus Christ can do His works and greater works because of the Holy Spirit indwelling them, which is in essence God and Christ indwelling them. They have the life of God within and so are activated by the Holy Spirit to speak the words of God and do the will of God as Jesus did. They are therefore as Jesus prophetic vessels of God in the world for the glory of His name and Kingdom.

"11 The Spirit of God, who raised Jesus from the dead, lives in you. And just as God raised Christ Jesus from the dead, he will give life to your mortal bodies by this same Spirit living within you" (Romans 8:11 NLT).

3. Have confidence that because they belong to Jesus, they are guaranteed anything they ask in his name "so that the Son can bring glory to the Father" (vs 13-14).

4. Understand that in order to live victorious lives in Christ, it is necessary to demonstrate love for God by obeying Him. When disciples of Jesus demonstrate their love for God by obeying His Commandments, they are rewarded as follows:
    -They are loved by the Father and Christ. Christ reveals himself to them.
    "Those who accept my commandments and obey them are the ones who love me. And because they love me, my Father will love them. And I will love   them

and reveal myself to each of them." (John 14:21 NLT).

>-They receive the Holy Spirit, a sign that they have not been abandoned by Christ.
> "If you love me, obey my commandments. 16 And I will ask the Father, and he will give you another Advocate, who will never leave you. 17 He is the Holy Spirit, who leads into all truth... No, I will not abandon you as orphans—I will come to you" (John 14:15-18 NLT).

>-They are loved by the Father. The Father and Christ "make their home" with the obedient. In other words the glorious presence of God abides with them forever.
> "Jesus replied, "All who love me will do what I say. My Father will love them, and we will come and make our home with each of them." (John 14:27NLT).

5. Live as children of God conscious of who the Holy Spirit is and his relevance as the power and Spirit of God in their lives. They therefore actively fellowship with the Holy Spirit;
Jesus said the "Holy Spirit—he will teach you everything and will remind you of everything I have told you. (John 14:26NLT).

6. Having received the Holy Spirit in their lives, they know that they have also simultaneously received "a gift—peace of mind and heart" and that this peace "is a gift the world cannot give" (vs 27).

7. As a believer of Christ, they must yield to God to transform them daily through His sanctification process so that they become more like Christ in terms of their nature or Character.
God's plan is that as Jesus' disciples are reconciled to Him they will increasingly become more like Him through becoming more like Christ. This is understandable because mankind is created by God in His image.

"that even though we were dead because of our sins, he gave us life when he raised Christ from the dead. (It is only by God's grace that you have been saved!) ⁶ For he raised us from the dead along with Christ and seated us with him in the heavenly realms because we are united with Christ Jesus. ⁷ So God can point to us in all future ages as examples of the incredible wealth of his grace and kindness toward us, as shown in all he has done for us who are united with Christ Jesus." (Eph. 2:5-7NLT).

II. "I AM THE BREAD OF LIFE".

"35 Jesus replied, I am the Bread of Life. Whoever comes to me will never be hungry again. Whoever believes in me will never be thirsty." (John 6:35NLT).

Jesus spoke about being the Bread of life after he discerned that the crowd were looking for him not because they believed in him or understood the miraculous signs, but because he had fed them with bread and fish.

When they found him, he advised them as follows " …don't be so concerned about perishable things like food. Spend your energy seeking the eternal life that the Son of Man can give you. For God the Father has given me the seal of his approval." (vs 27 NLT).

They had not believed yet, but they wanted to perform God's work. Jesus however said to them "This is the only work God wants from you: Believe in the one he has sent" (vs 29 NLT).

Jesus had just performed a miracle of multiplication of loaves and fish and fed a crowd of five thousand. They were among the crowd, yet they did not seem to realise he had done so for they said to him "Show us a miraculous sign if you want us to believe in you. What can you do?" (vs 30) It was a challenge for they said

"Moses gave them (their ancestors) bread to eat" (vs 31), they saw that as a miracle and wanted to know what Jesus could do. Jesus told them that it was Father God who gave their ancestors bread to eat from heaven and not Moses, Jesus added "and now he (God) offers you the true bread from heaven. The true bread of God is the one who comes down from heaven and gives life to the world" (vs 32-33).

Jesus had told them "don't be so concerned about perishable things like food." (vs 27) and also said that he is
-The source of the imperishable thing they need, eternal life. "Spend your energy seeking the eternal life that the Son of Man can give you. For God the Father has given me the seal of his approval."(vs 27)
-The true imperishable bread from heaven who gives life to the world being offered to the crowd (vs 32-33)
When they said they wanted this bread "every day" "35 Jesus replied, I am the Bread of Life. Whoever comes to me will never be hungry again. Whoever believes in me will never be thirsty. 36 But you haven't believed in me even though you have seen me. 37 However, those the Father has given me will come to me, and I will never reject them.

Jesus is totally devoted to caring for those who are predestined and become saved (his disciples), so that they remain in him and fulfil their destinies until he comes.

In verses 36 and 37, Jesus was stating what he knew to be true, which is that only those who the Father (God) has chosen even before the foundation of the earth, whose names are written in the Lamb's Book of Life will believe in him or come to him because God will send them. Jesus said "…and I will never reject them.38 For I have come down from heaven to do the will of God who sent me, not to do my own will.39 And this is the will of God, that I should not lose even one of all those he has given me, but that I should raise them up at the last day. 40 For it is my Father's will that all who see his Son and believe in him should have eternal life. I will raise them up at the last day." (vs 37-40).

Jesus as the Bread of Life

When Jesus said that he is the Bread of Life, he reveals his nature as
-Provider.
-A basic requirement for mankind to survive. Without him they will never be fulfilled or satisfied in their life path in terms of their identity and destiny. While natural food, as Manna in the wilderness given to the ancestors of his disciples, was not able to keep them alive, the person of Jesus as Lord and Saviour of someone is able to give one eternal life as well as the abundant or fulfilling life of God in their lives.

As the Bread of Life, Jesus was telling his disciples that he alone is able to quench their thirst and satisfy their hunger. Hunger and thirst in this context means the spiritual void within their inner most being in terms of their identity and destiny. This "hunger" and "thirst" can only be fulfilled by God Almighty through our Lord Jesus Christ because God and Jesus are abundant and eternal life-givers (John 10:10/John 3:16).

As Bread can be described as staple or a basic item of food, so too is the need to know one's identity and destiny a basic "hunger and thirst" of the human being. If only man would seek Jesus the bread of life as all they need for the fulfilment of their basic requirement in life, to know who they are and their purpose in life, they will never hunger or thirst for anything.

III. "I AM THE GOOD SHEPHERD" /"I AM THE GATE (DOOR)"

John 10:1-16:

"I tell you the truth, anyone who sneaks over the wall of a sheepfold, rather than going through the gate, must surely be a thief and a robber! ² But the one who enters through the gate is the shepherd of the sheep. ³ The gatekeeper opens the gate for him, and the sheep recognize his voice and come to him. He calls his own sheep by name and leads them out. ⁴ After he has gathered his own flock, he walks ahead of them, and they follow him because they know his voice. ⁵ They won't follow a stranger; they will run from him because they don't know his voice."

⁶ Those who heard Jesus use this illustration didn't understand what he meant, ⁷ so he explained it to them: "I tell you the truth, I am the gate for the sheep. ⁸ All who came before me were thieves and robbers. But the true sheep did not listen to them. ⁹ Yes, I am the gate. Those who come in through me will be saved. They will come and go freely and will find good pastures. ¹⁰ The thief's purpose is to steal and kill and destroy. My purpose is to give them a rich and satisfying life.

¹¹ "I am the good shepherd. The good shepherd sacrifices his life for the sheep. ¹² A hired hand will run when he sees a wolf coming. He will abandon the sheep because they don't belong to him and he isn't their shepherd. And so the wolf attacks them and scatters the flock. ¹³ The hired hand runs away because he's working only for the money and doesn't really care about the sheep.

¹⁴ "I am the good shepherd; I know my own sheep, and they know me,¹⁵ just as my Father knows me and I know the Father. So I sacrifice my life for the sheep. ¹⁶ I have other sheep, too, that are not in this sheepfold. I must bring them also. They will listen to my voice, and there will be one flock with one shepherd.(NLT)

As the Good Shepherd and Door, Jesus is revealed as
-Saviour
-Carer
-Protector
-Leader
-Gatherer
-Shelter (Sheepfold)
-Peace/Rest giver (where one finds "pasture").

Jesus expressed sacrificial loyalty and devotion to his disciples as

1. **A. The Good Shepherd.**

Jesus, the Good Shepherd,

- Knows his sheep.
- Searches for other sheep not yet in the sheepfold to bring them in (God's plan of salvation of multitudes through Christ is progressive).
- While the thief's purpose is to kill, steal and destroy, his is to give the sheep a rich and satisfying life.
- While a hired hand will run away when he sees a wolf coming because he does not care for the sheep as they are not his (and he only cares for the money), the Good Shepherd will not run away from his sheep when they are in danger, instead he protects them and sacrifices his life for them.

B. The Door or Gate.

Jesus describes himself as the only door or gate through whom man is saved and finds "pasture" or God's rest and provision.
"[7] so he explained it to them: "I tell you the truth, I am the gate for the sheep. [8] All who came before me were thieves and robbers. But the true sheep did not listen to them. [9] Yes, I am the gate. Those who come in through me will be saved. They will come and go freely and will find good pastures. [10] The thief's purpose is to steal and kill and destroy. My purpose is to give them a rich and satisfying life" (John 10:7-9 NLT).

2. As the Good Shepherd and Door, Jesus

- **describes the type of people who are his true Sheep:**
    - True disciples of Jesus are as loyal sheep; there is a depth of intimacy or oneness with Jesus which is the same as that between Jesus and the Father.

        As Jesus, the Good Shepherd knows his sheep, so they too know him, he calls them by name, leads them and they follow him alone and no one else because they recognise only his voice. This relationship is as the relationship between Jesus and Father God; the Father knows Jesus, just as Jesus knows the Father. The true sheep can distinguish between the voice of the Good Shepherd and that of the stranger or thieves and robbers and so will not follow them. The true 'sheep' (disciples) are therefore obedient to God's Word through Christ, and accept His guidance, commands and leading as sheep are reputed to do in relation to their master.

        In the Church, across denominations, characteristics of true sheep of the Good Shepherd as described in John 10 is the basis upon which God distinguishes between Jesus' true disciples and the false ones.

- **reveals that the gathering of his disciples or their unity is one of the goals of his mission.**
    - The intimacy or oneness with Christ as a lifestyle inevitably draws together all those who are true sheep of Christ because God's people are not supposed to walk alone. Jesus knows them individually by name and although he deals with them individually, he also deals with them collectively by gathering and leading them. As much as they know his voice, they also know one another.
    "He calls his own sheep by name and leads them out. [4] After he has gathered his own flock, he walks ahead of them, and they follow him because they know his voice." (John 10:3-4NLT).

CHAPTER 3

THE EIGHTH "I AM" SAYING: "I AM THE TRUE VINE"

"Yes, I am the vine; you are the branches…" (John 15:5NLT)

According to John 15, the disciples of Jesus are the Branches of the True Vine, Jesus.
The Father is the Vinedresser or Gardener or Husbandman.
The Father (Vinedresser) who sent Jesus (True Grapevine) is the one who decides who should be Jesus' disciple (Branch).

1. The True Vine and Branches.

Jesus said of himself:

"Yes, I am the vine; you are the branches. Those who remain in me, and I in them, will produce much fruit. For apart from me you can do nothing. ⁶ Anyone who does not remain in me is thrown away like a useless branch and withers. Such branches are gathered into a pile to be burned." (John 15:5-6 NLT).

i. The True Vine, Jesus "Good Tree" reproduces after himself, so his Branches manifest as bearers of fruit that last.

"You didn't choose me. I chose you. I appointed you to go and produce lasting fruit, so that the Father will give you whatever you ask for, using my name." (John 15:16 NLT).

The purpose of Jesus, the True Vine was to produce good fruit, because he is a "Good Tree".

Jesus said "A good tree produces good fruit, and a bad tree produces bad fruit. ¹⁸ A good tree can't produce bad fruit, and a bad tree can't produce good fruit. ¹⁹ So every tree that does not produce good fruit is chopped down and thrown into the fire. ²⁰ Yes, just as you can identify a tree by its fruit, so you can identify people by their actions."(Matthew 7:17-20 NLT).

The quality of the fruit is a sign that the tree reproduces after itself. A good tree does not produce bad fruit. They will be known by the fruit they produce. Jesus (True Vine) is the good tree that produces good fruit. If his followers are true disciples or "Branches" then it is inevitable that they would accept nourishment from him, the "good tree" and also produce good fruit.

If someone says that they are Christ's (abiding in the True Vine) but are not focused on being fruitful Branches of the True Vine, then they are deceiving themselves and others. The life of Father (Vinedresser) through Jesus (True Vine) enables Jesus' disciples (Branches) to live a life that they were predestined to live by the Father and so they are productive for His glory as they fulfil their destinies founded on the principles of God's kingdom.

The lives of believers in Jesus must reflect his. This is why the Apostle Paul encouraged the Ephesian believers to "put on Christ":

"For you are all children of God through faith in Christ Jesus. ²⁷ And all who have been united with Christ in baptism have put on Christ, like putting on new clothes. (Galatians 3:26-27 NLT).

ii. The Powerful "Key" of Obedience.

- **The key to being loved by Father and living in His abiding presence or glory is obedience.**

It is only those who obey the Father through Jesus, the Son by receiving God's Word and living by it who have the abiding presence or glory of God. They have access to all that Father has predestined for them before creation.

Those who accept my commandments and obey them are the ones who love me. And because they love me, my Father will love them. And I will love them and reveal myself to each of them." ²² Judas (not Judas Iscariot, but the other disciple with that name) said to him, "Lord, why are you going to reveal yourself only to us and not to the world at large?" ²³ Jesus replied, "All who love me will do what I say. My Father will love them, and we will come and make our home with each of them." (John 14:21-23 NLT).

- **Rewards gained from obeying the command to love one another.**

A key command requiring obedience which reaps fruitfulness & the gift of revelation is for believers to love one another as Jesus loved them and laid down his life for them.

Obedience results in

- a special relationship of intimate friendship between the True Vine & Branches.
- The gift of revelation knowledge of Father imparted from Jesus.
  "¹² This is my commandment: Love each other in the same way I have loved you. ¹³ There is no greater love than to lay down one's life for one's friends. ¹⁴ You are my friends if you do what I command. ¹⁵ I no longer call you slaves, because a master doesn't confide in his slaves. Now you are my friends, since I have told you everything the Father told me. ¹⁶ You didn't choose me. I chose you. I appointed you to go and produce lasting fruit, so that the Father will give you whatever you ask for, using my name. ¹⁷ This is my command: Love each other. (John 15:12-17 NLT)

- **Obeying commands of Jesus results in fruitfulness and avoids being cut off from the True Vine, Jesus.**

"Remain in me, and I will remain in you. For a branch cannot produce fruit if it is severed from the vine, and you cannot be fruitful unless you remain in me. **5** "Yes, I am the vine; you are the branches. Those who remain in me, and I in them, will produce much fruit. For apart from me you can do nothing. **6** Anyone who does not remain in me is thrown away like a useless branch and withers. Such branches are gathered into a pile to be burned. **7** But if you remain in me and my words remain in you, you may ask for anything you want, and it will be granted! **8** When you produce much fruit, you are my true disciples. This brings great glory to my Father. **9** "I have loved you even as the Father has loved me. Remain in my love. **10** When you obey my commandments, you remain in my love, just as I obey my Father's commandments and remain in his love." (John 15:4-10 NLT).

iii. The chosen among the called Branches who abide in the True Vine are those who will stay with Jesus Christ regardless of the consequences.

A true disciple is one who is willing to share in Jesus' suffering; "Anyone who eats my flesh and drinks my blood remains in me and I in him" (John 6:57).

"**28** They replied, "We want to perform God's works, too. What should we do?" **29** Jesus told them, "This is the only work God wants from you: Believe in the one he has sent."**30** They answered, "Show us a miraculous sign if you want us to believe in you. What can you do? **31** After all, our ancestors ate manna while they journeyed through the wilderness! The Scriptures say, 'Moses gave them bread from heaven to eat.'"**32** Jesus said, "I tell you the truth, Moses didn't give you bread from heaven. My Father did. And now he offers you the true bread from heaven.

33 The true bread of God is the one who comes down from heaven and gives life to the world." **34** "Sir," they said, "give us that bread every day." **35** Jesus replied, "I am the bread of life. Whoever comes to me will never be hungry again. Whoever believes in me will never be thirsty. **36** But you haven't believed in me even though you have seen me. ³⁷ However, those the Father has given me will come to me, and I will never reject them. ³⁸ For I have come down from heaven to do the will of God who sent me, not to do my own will.

³⁹ And this is the will of God, that I should not lose even one of all those he has given me, but that I should raise them up at the last day. ⁴⁰ For it is my Father's will that all who see his Son and believe in him should have eternal life. I will raise them up at the last day." ⁴¹ Then the people began to murmur in disagreement because he had said, "I am the bread that came down from heaven." ⁴² They said, "Isn't this Jesus, the son of Joseph? We know his father and mother. How can he say, 'I came down from heaven'?" ⁴³ But Jesus replied, "Stop complaining about what I said. ⁴⁴ For no one can come to me unless the Father who sent me draws them to me, and at the last day I will raise them up.

⁴⁵ As it is written in the Scriptures, 'They will all be taught by God.' Everyone who listens to the Father and learns from him comes to me. ⁴⁶ (Not that anyone has ever seen the Father; only I, who was sent from God, have seen him.) ⁴⁷ "I tell you the truth, anyone who believes has eternal life. ⁴⁸ Yes, I am the bread of life! ⁴⁹ Your ancestors ate manna in the wilderness, but they all died. ⁵⁰ Anyone who eats the bread from heaven, however, will never die. ⁵¹ I am the living bread that came down from heaven. Anyone who eats this bread will live forever; and this bread, which I will offer so the world may live, is my flesh." ⁵² Then the people began arguing with each other about what he meant. "How can this man give us his flesh to eat?" they asked. ⁵³ So Jesus said again, "I tell you the truth, unless you eat the flesh of the Son of Man and drink his blood, you cannot have eternal life within you. ⁵⁴ But anyone who eats my flesh and drinks my blood has eternal life, and I will raise that person at the last day. ⁵⁵ For my flesh is true food, and my blood is true drink.

⁵⁶ Anyone who eats my flesh and drinks my blood remains in me, and I in him. ⁵⁷ I live because of the living Father who sent me; in the same way, anyone who feeds on me will live because of me. ⁵⁸ I am the true bread that came down from heaven. Anyone

who eats this bread will not die as your ancestors did (even though they ate the manna) but will live forever." [59] He said these things while he was teaching in the synagogue in Capernaum. (John 6:28-59 NLT).

Jesus spoke boldly about those who were candidates for eternal life; those who ate his flesh and drank his blood. He was speaking of those who believed that he was the Saviour of the world through the act of his death, burial and resurrection. In his death his body was beaten and pierced with nails upon a cross, this resulted in blood draining out of his body. Therefore those who believe that this act of death was sacrificial, are in effect aligning themselves with Jesus' suffering and accept whatever happens to them including suffering for his sake.

Jesus spoke realistically to his disciples that they will be persecuted as he was:

[18] "If the world hates you, remember that it hated me first. [19] The world would love you as one of its own if you belonged to it, but you are no longer part of the world. I chose you to come out of the world, so it hates you. [20] Do you remember what I told you? 'A slave is not greater than the master.' Since they persecuted me, naturally they will persecute you. And if they had listened to me, they would listen to you. [21] They will do all this to you because of me, for they have rejected the one who sent me. [22] They would not be guilty if I had not come and spoken to them. But now they have no excuse for their sin. [23] Anyone who hates me also hates my Father. [24] If I hadn't done such miraculous signs among them that no one else could do, they would not be guilty. But as it is, they have seen everything I did, yet they still hate me and my Father. [25] This fulfills what is written in their Scriptures: 'They hated me without cause.' (John 15:18-25 NLT).

The Apostle Paul expressed his total devotion to Christ in this manner:

"Yes, everything else is worthless when compared with the infinite value of knowing Christ Jesus my Lord. For his sake I have discarded everything else, counting it all as garbage, so that I could gain Christ 9 and become one with him. I no longer count on my own righteousness through obeying the law; rather, I become righteous through faith in Christ. For God's way of making us right with himself depends on faith. 10 I want to know Christ and experience the mighty power that raised him from the dead. I want to suffer with him, sharing in his death, 11 so that one way or another I will experience the resurrection from the dead!" (Philippians 3:8-11 NLT).

iv. Disbelief and rejection of Jesus.

"60 Many of his disciples said, "This is very hard to understand. How can anyone accept it?" 61 Jesus was aware that his disciples were complaining, so he said to them, "Does this offend you? 62 Then what will you think if you see the Son of Man ascend to heaven again? 63 The Spirit alone gives eternal life. Human effort accomplishes nothing. And the very words I have spoken to you are spirit and life. 64 But some of you do not believe me." (For Jesus knew from the beginning which ones didn't believe, and he knew who would betray him.) 65 Then he said, "That is why I said that people can't come to me unless the Father gives them to me." 66 At this point many of his disciples turned away and deserted him." (John 6:60-66 NLT).

There were many who were called as disciples of Jesus, but on hearing his speech about his pending death and his expectations of them, they deserted him. Many either did not understand what he meant because of the manner in which he spoke (i.e. eat his flesh and drink his blood) and concluded he was not in his right mind or if they managed to understand what he said, they still felt

- that what he said about his pending death was untrue,
- offended by the fact that he was literally asking them to eat his flesh and drink his blood.

Those who were offended to the point of turning away from Jesus permanently were not meant to remain his disciples anyway. Why? This is because they were, as Judas, not chosen by the Father (John 6:65) to fulfil the course of their walk with Jesus. Jesus knew (John 6:64) from the beginning which of his followers at that time did not believe in him and the one who would betray him (Judas).

2. The Vinedresser, God the Father

i. When abiding in the True Vine, the Father (Vinedresser) prunes or purges the fruitful Branches so that they produce more fruit & discards the fruitless ones.

God the Father knows those who are truly His, and knows that they are the ones who will bear fruit as they are the ones who abide in the True Vine, Jesus. They are therefore the ones the Vinedresser planned before the foundation of the earth to prune or purge so that they produce more fruit.

The Father engages in His task as a Vinedresser; taking away Branches that do not bear fruit and pruning or purging the Branches that do so that they will bear more fruit. Jesus said of the Father, the Vinedresser: "He cuts off every branch of mine that doesn't produce fruit, and he prunes the branches that do bear fruit so they will produce even more." (John 15: 2 NLT).

The will of God the Father (Vinedresser) through the Son (True Vine) is always communicated to the disciple (Branch) who abides in the Son (True Vine). The disciple who listens and obeys will receive favour from God:

    -The fulfilment of God's will in their lives.

    -Natural and spiritual blessings, which include God's presence and answers to their prayers according to the will of God. They will therefore bear fruit because their desires are aligned with the will of the Father.

It is not surprising that Jesus included in the "Lord's Prayer" (Matthew 6:9-13) "Thy kingdom come, thy will be done on earth as it is in heaven" (vs 10, KJV). As the True Vine came to do the will of the Father, so his disciples, the Branches must seek His will and do it. Obedience to God's will makes a way for victorious Christian living.

ii. The Vinedresser, Abba Father assures abundant fruitfulness for true disciples (Branches) of Jesus.

- The Vinedresser's will is that all should bear abundant fruit through the Son and He responds to those who do because
  i. He is a rewarder of those who sincerely seek him (Hebrews 11:6).
  ii. He is faithful to His covenant promises to mankind.

- The Vinedresser's will is that all should bear abundant fruit through the Son and He works through His Spirit for this to happen. This is why Jesus told his disciples that when he goes away he will pray to the Father to send them the helper, the Holy Spirit (John 14:16). The Holy Spirit is fundamentally the power of God, and is also known as the Spirit of Truth and Prophecy and is the testimony of Jesus (Rev 19:10/John 16:13/John 15:26) and reminds believers in Jesus of his teachings (John 14:26) among other functions. When the Holy Spirit indwells a believer in Jesus it means Jesus is within them this is why they can be productive or fruitful in this world to the glory of God.

Jesus spoke of the fact that those who abide in him will be endowed with great power from God that they would not only do his miraculous works but even greater works than he did.

"I tell you the truth, anyone who believes in me will do the same works I have done, and even greater works, because I am going to be with the Father. (John 14:12 NLT).
Regarding those who do his works, Jesus said "[18] They will be able to handle snakes with safety, and if they drink anything poisonous, it won't hurt them…" (Mark 16:18 NLT).
"I no longer call you slaves, because a master doesn't confide in his slaves. Now you are my friends, since I have told you everything the Father told me. [16] You didn't choose me. I chose you. I appointed you to go and produce lasting fruit, so that the Father will give you whatever you ask for, using my name. [17] This is my command: Love each other." (John 15:15-18 NLT).

Even though Jesus was speaking to his disciples then and in the future when he spoke the above verses (John 15:15-18), the fact that he was physically with the disciples then means that they were able to cultivate friendship with him. However, Jesus' disciples of today can only remain his friends if they fellowship with the Holy Spirit he prayed for Father God to send before he departed the earth physically. The Holy Spirit bears witness to Jesus, empowers, teaches and reveals the will of God to believers in Jesus. The Holy Spirit therefore imparts the life of God within believers in Jesus Christ and bears witness with their spirits that they are children of God (more on Holy Spirit, see Chapter 1).

"So you have not received a spirit that makes you fearful slaves. Instead, you received God's Spirit when he adopted you as his own children. Now we call him, "Abba, Father." (Romans 8:15 NLT).
The Holy Spirit, the Spirit and power of God, knows the will of

God and reveals it to God's children so that they are able to live godly lives.

"You are controlled by the Spirit if you have the Spirit of God living in you. (And remember that those who do not have the Spirit of Christ living in them do not belong to him at all.) [10] And Christ lives within you, so even though your body will die because of sin, the Spirit gives you life because you have been made right with God. [11] The Spirit of God, who raised Jesus from the dead, lives in you. And just as God raised Christ Jesus from the dead, he will give life to your mortal bodies by this same Spirit living within you." (Romans 8:9-11NLT).

iii. Abba Father is not only the Vinedresser, pruning the fruitful Branches of the True Vine, He also determines who should be a Branch.

Father determines who will come to Jesus or believe in him. Many deserted him as expressed in the account in John 6:60-66 because they refused to accept what he said. The truth of the matter is that it was Father who did not allow them to accept Jesus' words because they were not marked for salvation (John 6:65).

"[44] For no one can come to me unless the Father who sent me draws them to me, and at the last day I will raise them up" (John 6:44 NLT). Judas stayed with Jesus until the appointed time of his betrayal of Jesus.

"[67] Then Jesus turned to the Twelve and asked, "Are you also going to leave?" [68] Simon Peter replied, "Lord, to whom would we go? You have the words that give eternal life. [69] We believe, and we know you are the Holy One of God." [70] Then Jesus said, "I chose the twelve of you, but one is a devil." [71] He was speaking of Judas, son of Simon Iscariot, one of the Twelve, who would later betray him." (John 6:67-71 NLT).

iv. Jesus' disciples (Branches) are appointed to bear fruit that will remain.

Bearing fruit is living a life which demonstrates that one is a Branch of the True Vine and is being nourished by the True Vine, meaning they are receiving the Word of Truth and the life of God through Bible study, meditation and fellowship with the Holy Spirit. They live a life of prayer and praise unto God. In so doing, they are able to communicate with Father and know his will as "friends" of Jesus according to John 15:15.

As a result God the Father, the Vinedresser responds in love (John 14:21-26) by pruning the Branch so that it bears more fruit (John 15:1-6). Father God therefore governs one's life as a response to one's willingness to not only accept Jesus Christ as Lord and Saviour but to actively live a life abiding in Him through obeying His commands, which in effect means one is obeying God, because God and Jesus Christ are one.

WHAT IS GODLY FRUIT THAT REMAINS?

a) Doing the works of Jesus and greater works.

> "I tell you the truth, anyone who believes in me will do the same works I have done, and even greater works, because I am going to be with the Father." (John 14:12 NLT).

b) Fulfilling one's destiny as blessed to be a blessing to multitudes.

> "4 Remain in me, and I will remain in you....Those who remain in me, and I in them, will produce much fruit. For apart from me you can do nothing." (John 15:4-5 NLT).

c) Knowing the will of Father progressively through abiding in Him and as a result desiring and praying His will so as to obtain answers to one's prayers to the glory of His name and kingdom.

"But if you remain in me and my words remain in you, you may ask for anything you want, and it will be granted!8 When you produce much fruit, you are my true disciples. This brings great glory to my Father… 16 You didn't choose me. I chose you. I appointed you to go and produce lasting fruit, so that the Father will give you whatever you ask for, using my name." (John 15:7-8, 16 NLT).

v. The Vinedresser is always at the fruitful disciple's service.

The Vinedresser, Father God will always be at one's service if one abides in the True Vine to ensure that one is progressively more fruitful and the bearer of lasting fruit. This should encourage those who are consistently living a committed Christian life. Their gift from the Vinedresser is consistent pruning or purging so that they will progressively become more Holy or consecrated (set apart) as He is holy.

" But now you must be holy in everything you do, just as God who chose you is holy. ¹⁶ For the Scriptures say, "You must be holy because I am holy." (1 Peter 1:15-16 NLT).

God is obviously not the source of evil, but He uses trials and afflictions His children undergo to prune them. Chastening is used by God in the pruning process and can involve suffering.

In Hebrews 12:6, we read that God chastens those He loves. He is always with His people in their trials and tribulations and outworks His divine strategies for their good (Romans 8:28).

In James 1:2-4 (NLT) we read about the benefits of trials:

"Dear brothers and sisters, when troubles of any kind come your way, consider it an opportunity for great joy. For you know that when your faith is tested, your endurance has a chance to grow. So let it grow, for when your endurance is fully developed, you will be perfect and complete, needing nothing."

God's goal for pruning or chastening His people is that they would respond to the conviction of the Holy Spirit, repent from their sins and receive transformation of heart so that they are able to live consecrated lives unto God.

Encouragement

Obedience to God is the gateway to fruitfulness…

The obedience to the commands of Jesus sets one on course to becoming a fruitful disciple "Branch" who is pruned by the Vinedresser (God the Father) to produce more fruit.

If people say they are obedient to God and abide in Jesus Christ and yet they are not bearing fruit as expected then there is something wrong; either they

- are lying and pretending to live a committed Christian life or
- are genuinely deceived, thinking they are in the truth, but actually their understanding of how to live a Christian life is flawed at the root,
- have generational demonic strongholds or curses which
- are preventing them from bearing fruit as is expected of people who as far as they know are doing all they can to live for the Lord.

Seeking God in prayer to change one's situation will result in his gracious process of deliverance which will certainly begin with God revealing which of the three points mentioned apply, if not all of them. Responding adequately to God's revelation for the purpose of redemption will result in breakthrough and ultimate fruitfulness to the glory of His name.

CHAPTER 4

JESUS CHRIST, THE ALL-SEEING AND ALL-KNOWING GOD AND PROPHET

His All-Seeing and All-Knowing nature gives an insight into Jesus Christ as the All-Powerful God and Prophet.

Jesus is God and was therefore all-powerful during his ministry on earth, however having come in bodily form as a man he exerted his power within the confines of his mission. This meant that while he could prevent certain things happening to him, for instance being beaten, mocked and crucified, he allowed himself to go through it all because of his ultimate purpose which was to die and be raised on the third day to redeem man from sin (John 3:16/ 2 Corinthians 5:19). His mighty power was also demonstrated in many ways such as healings and casting out demons from the demon possessed.

Jesus' life on earth was as a Prophet, he lived according to how God wanted to manifest himself on earth, so Jesus the Son of Man was an instrument through whom God worked to fulfil his redemptive plan and to communicate this plan to mankind. This is why Jesus said that he only did what he saw Father God doing, was exercising His authority when he worked or that it was Father working through him.

As the instrument for the fulfilment of God's will on earth, Jesus the Son of Man was revealed to be the all-seeing and all-knowing God as he walked on earth with men. These are some of the reasons why this was important. He could

- Communicate with individuals on a one on one basis and collectively in effective
ways (i.e. teachings directly and using parables) for the sake of their redemption because he had an insight into the

condition of their hearts or lives and knew what they needed from him.

- ensure that that he was fulfilling each stage of his time on earth under God's terms
and not on man's terms. For instance when he had foreknowledge of what man intended for him at any given time, if he knew that it was not God's will for him, he was able to prevent it from happening.

PART 1 GENERAL EXAMPLES OF HOW JESUS WAS ALL-KNOWING/ALL-SEEING.

Jesus foreknew

1. **Nathanael would become his disciple even before Philip called him.**

Jesus also knew Nathanael's heart condition as "an Israelite in whom there is no guile" meaning an Israelite who had a pure heart (John 1:47-48).

2. **his own God ordained purpose. In conversation with Nathanael, at the beginning of his ministry, Jesus gave a picture of himself as a supernaturally powerful person.**

When Jesus said to Nathanael
"…Do you believe this just because I told you I had seen you under the fig tree? You will see greater things than this." Then he said, "I tell you the truth, you will all see heaven open and the angels of God going up and down on the Son of Man, the one who is the stairway between heaven and earth" (John 1:50-51 NLT).

When Jesus said the aforementioned, he was giving a sign of what his ministry would entail, it was as though he was saying, "I don't only have foreknowledge about what people will or will not do but I also have foreknowledge of my own God ordained purpose and will. You will see in my ministerial life angels ascending and descending upon me "The Son of man".

What did "angels ascending and descending" mean? Jesus gave a picture of himself, at the beginning of his ministry as a supernatural person with the spiritual power of God as a Prophet and a Priest or intercessor.

- **PRIEST/INTERCESSOR;** "angels ascending" He would communicate with the Father for the sake of mankind as a priest or intercessor on their behalf. This speaks of Christ Jesus as a
  - Sacrificial Lamb who was slain to takes away the sins of the world (John 1:9), as well as the
  - High Priest who made a once and for all sacrifice (through his identity as a sacrificial Lamb) to make atonement for the sins of mankind.

"Unlike those other high priests, he does not need to offer sacrifices everyday They did this for their own sins first and then for the sins of the people. But Jesus did this once for all when he offered himself as the sacrifice for the people's sins." (Hebrews 7:27 NLT).

- **PROPHET;** "angels descending" He would receive revelation from the Father to impart to mankind.

He came to fulfil Father's will, so he would do and say only what Father told him to do and say. All one needs to do to become a child of God is to confess with their mouth and believe in their hearts that Jesus Christ is Lord and they will be saved and accepted into the kingdom of God.

"For this is how God loved the world: He gave his one and only Son, so that everyone who believes in him will not perish but have eternal life" (John 3:16 NLT).

"If you openly declare that Jesus is Lord and believe in your heart that God raised him from the dead, you will be saved. For it is by believing in your heart that you are made right with God, and it is by openly declaring your faith that you are saved." (Romans 10:9-10 NLT).

Jesus Christ is therefore the only means to access God the creator. Jesus said about himself "I am the way, the truth, and the life. No one can come to the Father except through me" (John 14:6 NLT).

Jesus Christ is the means through whom anyone can be reconciled to God and also be able to access the revelatory realm of God or the "Portals of Heaven" The scripture "We are more than conquerors through him who loves us" (Romans 8:37) becomes a reality only if believers in Christ allow God to sanctify them through daily fellowship with Him (bible study, prayer and living a worshipful life unto Him), in the Spirit. The degree of sanctification is dependent on the degree of daily surrender to God.

When the priestly (intercessory) and prophetic nature of Christ among other attributes of his become increasingly the nature of the believer who is in true fellowship, then it means they are in oneness with Christ and have the conqueror's anointing through their God given authority. When they exercise their authority in Christ breakthroughs and victories manifest to the glory of God.

In Matthew 13:57 (also mentioned by Apostles Mark and Luke), when Jesus was rejected in Nazareth by people who knew his family and saw him growing up, he refers to himself as a Prophet;

"…Then Jesus told them "A prophet is honoured everywhere except in his own hometown and among his own family. And so he did only a few miracles there because of their unbelief." (Matthew 13:57 -58 NLT).

3. **from the beginning those who would not believe his words and also the one (Judas Iscariot) who would betray him.**

"⁵³ So Jesus said again, "I tell you the truth, unless you eat the flesh of the Son of Man and drink his blood, you cannot have eternal life within you. ⁵⁴ But anyone who eats my flesh and drinks my blood has eternal life, and I will raise that person at the last day. ⁵⁵ For my flesh is true food, and my blood is true drink. ⁵⁶ Anyone who eats my flesh and drinks my blood remains in me, and I in him. ⁵⁷ I live because of the living Father who sent me; in the same way, anyone who feeds on me will live because of me. ⁵⁸ I am the true bread that came down from heaven. Anyone who eats this bread will not die as your ancestors did (even though they ate the manna) but will live forever."

⁵⁹ He said these things while he was teaching in the synagogue in Capernaum.⁶⁰ Many of his disciples said, "This is very hard to understand. How can anyone accept it?"

⁶¹ Jesus was aware that his disciples were complaining, so he said to them, "Does this offend you? ⁶² Then what will you think if you see the Son of Man ascend to heaven again? ⁶³ The Spirit alone gives eternal life. Human effort accomplishes nothing. And the very words I have spoken to you are spirit and life. ⁶⁴ But some of you do not believe me." (For Jesus knew from the beginning which ones didn't believe, and he knew who would betray him.) ⁶⁵ Then he said, "That is why I said that people can't come to me unless the Father gives them to me." (John 6:53-65 NLT).

4. when his disciples did not understand what he said.

"¹⁵ All that belongs to the Father is mine; this is why I said, 'The Spirit will tell you whatever he receives from me.' ¹⁶ "In a little while you won't see me anymore. But a little while after that, you will see me again."¹⁷ Some of the disciples asked each other, "What does he mean when he says, 'In a little while you won't see me, but then you will see me,' and 'I am going to the Father'? ¹⁸ And what does he mean by 'a little while'? We don't understand."

¹⁹ Jesus realized they wanted to ask him about it, so he said, "Are you asking yourselves what I meant? I said in a little while you won't see me, but a little while after that you will see me again. ²⁰ I tell you the truth, you will weep and mourn over what is going to happen to me, but the world will rejoice. You will grieve, but your

grief will suddenly turn to wonderful joy. ²¹ It will be like a woman suffering the pains of labor. When her child is born, her anguish gives way to joy because she has brought a new baby into the world. ²² So you have sorrow now, but I will see you again; then you will rejoice, and no one can rob you of that joy."(John 16:15-22 NLT).

5. **when his hour had come for him to be betrayed, die and then depart to Father.**

"Before the Passover celebration, Jesus knew that his hour had come to leave this world and return to his Father. He had loved his disciples during his ministry on earth, and now he loved them to the very end.² It was time for supper, and the devil had already prompted Judas, son of Simon Iscariot, to betray Jesus. ³ Jesus knew that the Father had given him authority over everything and that he had come from God and would return to God. ⁴ So he got up from the table, took off his robe, wrapped a towel around his waist" (John 13:1-4 NLT).

6. **the precise day and time when one of his disciples (Judas Iscariot) would betray him. When God's appointed time came Jesus provoked that disciple into action.**

"¹⁰ Jesus replied, "A person who has bathed all over does not need to wash, except for the feet, to be entirely clean. And you disciples are clean, but not all of you." ¹¹ For Jesus knew who would betray him. That is what he meant when he said, "Not all of you are clean... ¹⁸ "I am not saying these things to all of you; I know the ones I have chosen. But this fulfils the Scripture that says, 'The one who eats my food has turned against me.' ¹⁹ I tell you this beforehand, so that when it happens you will believe that I AM the Messiah.²⁰ I tell you the truth, anyone who welcomes my messenger is welcoming me, and anyone who welcomes me is welcoming the Father who sent me."
²¹ Now Jesus was deeply troubled, and he exclaimed, "I tell you the truth, one of you will betray me!"²² The disciples looked at each other, wondering whom he could mean.²³ The disciple Jesus loved was sitting next to Jesus at the table.²⁴ Simon Peter motioned to him to ask, "Who's he talking about?" ²⁵ So that disciple leaned over to Jesus and asked, "Lord, who is it?"²⁶ Jesus responded, "It is the one to whom I give the bread I dip in the bowl." And when he had dipped it, he gave it to Judas,

son of Simon Iscariot. ²⁷ When Judas had eaten the bread, Satan entered into him. Then Jesus told him, "Hurry and do what you're going to do." ²⁸ None of the others at the table knew what Jesus meant. ²⁹ Since Judas was their treasurer, some thought Jesus was telling him to go and pay for the food or to give some money to the poor. ³⁰ So Judas left at once, going out into the night.
³¹ As soon as Judas left the room, Jesus said, "The time has come for the Son of Man to enter into his glory, and God will be glorified because of him. ³² And since God receives glory because of the Son, he will give his own glory to the Son, and he will do so at once." (John 13:10-11, 18-32 NLT).

7. **all things that were to happen to him i.e. when the soldiers of chief priests came with Judas to arrest him. He therefore allowed himself to be taken by the soldiers.**

"After saying these things, Jesus crossed the Kidron Valley with his disciples and entered a grove of olive trees. ² Judas, the betrayer, knew this place, because Jesus had often gone there with his disciples. ³ The leading priests and Pharisees had given Judas a contingent of Roman soldiers and Temple guards to accompany him. Now with blazing torches, lanterns, and weapons, they arrived at the olive grove.
⁴ Jesus fully realized all that was going to happen to him, so he stepped forward to meet them. "Who are you looking for?" he asked. ⁵ "Jesus the Nazarene," they replied. "I AM he," Jesus said. (Judas, who betrayed him, was standing with them.)" (John 18:1-5 NLT).

8. **that Peter would betray him after he was captured.**

Jesus assured his disciples that they would go where he was going. He however let Peter know that while Peter thought he was ready to lay his life down for Jesus in reality Peter was not ready.

"³⁶ Simon Peter asked, "Lord, where are you going?" And Jesus replied, "You can't go with me now, but you will follow me later."
³⁷ "But why can't I come now, Lord?" he asked. "I'm ready to die

for you. Jesus answered, "Die for me? I tell you the truth, Peter - before the rooster crows tomorrow morning, you will deny three times that you even know me".(John 13:36-37 NLT).

Jesus' prophecy about Peter's denial was fulfilled:

a) Denial of Jesus by Peter - First time.

"Simon Peter followed Jesus, as did another of the disciples. That other disciple was acquainted with the high priest, so he was allowed to enter the high priest's courtyard with Jesus. ¹⁶ Peter had to stay outside the gate. Then the disciple who knew the high priest spoke to the woman watching at the gate, and she let Peter in. ¹⁷ The woman asked Peter, "You're not one of that man's disciples, are you?" "No," he said, "I am not.""(John 18:15-17 NLT).

b) Denial of Jesus by Peter - Second time.

"Then Annas bound Jesus and sent him to Caiaphas, the high priest. ²⁵ Meanwhile, as Simon Peter was standing by the fire warming himself, they asked him again, "You're not one of his disciples, are you?" He denied it, saying, "No, I am not."" (John 18:24-25 NLT).

c) Denial of Jesus by Peter - Third time.

"²⁶ But one of the household slaves of the high priest, a relative of the man whose ear Peter had cut off, asked, "Didn't I see you out there in the olive grove with Jesus?" ²⁷ Again Peter denied it. And immediately a rooster crowed." (John18:26-27 NLT).

Jesus knows of the process of transformation a believer in him needs to the point where they become bold enough to confess openly that they are believers in him when faced with persecution or possible murder.

They need to overcome the fear of what people will say, fear of loss of reputation and fear of persecution and death. This is a process and the degree and timing of differs from person to person.

Dependence on God for deliverance from fear is necessary, first one has to acknowledge and confess their sin of fearfulness as Peter did after the cock crowed the third time. In so doing the power of God's forgiveness through Jesus' sacrificial death will be activated and a way made by God for deliverance and healing, or cleansing from all unrighteousness according to 1 John 1:9. Thus by the power of the cross, the spirit of fear is exchanged for the Spirit of boldness.

Such boldness is the manifestation of a Christ-like nature of sacrificial living and fearlessness for the purposes of God. Peter overcame and became a Spirit-filled Apostle who preached the message of salvation boldly and was raised by God to perform miracles.

9. **the precise time for him to draw his last breath while on the cross; at the time when all things in scripture was accomplished.**

"[28] Jesus knew that his mission was now finished, and to fulfil Scripture he said, "I am thirsty." [29] A jar of sour wine was sitting there, so they soaked a sponge in it, put it on a hyssop branch, and held it up to his lips. [30] When Jesus had tasted it, he said, "It is finished!" Then he bowed his head and released his spirit. (John 19:28-30 NLT).

PART 2

JESUS WAS CAUTIOUS BECAUSE HE HAD FOREKNOWLEDGE OF THE CONDITION OF MAN'S HEART.

1. **He did not allow himself to be subject to man for he knew the condition of man's heart.**

People saw Jesus' miraculous signs and some believed in him, however he did not allow himself to be subject to man because he knew the condition of a man's heart.

"23 Because of the miraculous signs Jesus did in Jerusalem at the Passover celebration, many began to trust in him. 24 But Jesus didn't trust them, because he knew all about people. 25 No one needed to tell him about human nature, for he knew what was in each person's heart." (John 2:23-25 NLT).

2. To prevent attempts to control his destiny, Jesus slipped away from the crowd.

After performing a miracle or being in a crowd for a time, Jesus had a tendency to slip away either into the crowd or go a distance away on his own so that people will not know where he was. This is because he did not want to subject himself to them so that they would attempt to control his destiny.

i. He chose to be inconspicuous and be among people only when it was absolutely necessary; After Jesus healed the paralyzed man at the pool of Bethesda, and told him to pick up his mat and walk, Jesus slipped away into the crowd.

"Afterward Jesus returned to Jerusalem for one of the Jewish holy days. 2 Inside the city, near the Sheep Gate, was the pool of Bethesda, with five covered porches. 3 Crowds of sick people—blind, lame, or paralyzed—lay on the porches. 5 One of the men lying there had been sick for thirty-eight years. 6 When Jesus saw him and knew he had been ill for a long time, he asked him, "Would you like to get well?" 7 "I can't, sir," the sick man said, "for I have no one to put me into the pool when the water bubbles up. Someone else always gets there ahead of me." 8 Jesus told him, "Stand up, pick up your mat, and walk!" 9 Instantly, the man was healed! He rolled up his sleeping mat and began walking! But this miracle happened on the Sabbath,

10 so the Jewish leaders objected. They said to the man who was cured, "You can't work on the Sabbath! The law doesn't allow you to carry that sleeping mat!" 11 But he replied, "The man who healed me told me,

'Pick up your mat and walk.'" 12 "Who said such a thing as that?" they demanded. 13 The man didn't know, for Jesus had disappeared into the crowd. 14 But afterward Jesus found him in the Temple and told him, "Now you are well; so stop sinning, or something even worse may happen to you." (John 5:1-14 NLT).

ii. He did not want to be made king by force: After multiplying five loaves and two small fish at the sea of Tiberias, he departed to be alone.

"When the people saw him do this miraculous sign, they exclaimed, "Surely, he is the Prophet we have been expecting!" 15 When Jesus saw that they were ready to force him to be their king, he slipped away into the hills by himself." (John 6:14-15 NLT).

iii. Jesus journeyed to the Feast of Tabernacles in secret. He avoided being placed in situations where he would suffer a premature death by being killed before the time set by God for his crucifixion.

"After this, Jesus travelled around Galilee. He wanted to stay out of Judea, where the Jewish leaders were plotting his death. 2 But soon it was time for the Jewish Festival of Shelters, 3 and Jesus' brothers said to him, "Leave here and go to Judea, where your followers can see your miracles! 4 You can't become famous if you hide like this! If you can do such wonderful things, show yourself to the world!" 5 For even his brothers didn't believe in him.
6 Jesus replied, "Now is not the right time for me to go, but you can go anytime. 7 The world can't hate you, but it does hate me because I accuse it of doing evil. 8 You go on. I'm not going to this festival, because my time has not yet come." 9 After saying these things, Jesus remained in Galilee.10 But after his brothers left for the festival, Jesus also went, though secretly, staying out of public view.

11 The Jewish leaders tried to find him at the festival and kept asking if anyone had seen him. 12 There was a lot of grumbling about him among the crowds. Some argued, "He's a good man," but others said, "He's nothing but a fraud who deceives the people." 13 But no one had the courage to speak favorably about him in public, for they were afraid of getting in trouble with the Jewish leaders. 14 Then, midway through the festival, Jesus went up to the Temple and began to teach. 15 The people

were surprised when they heard him. "How does he know so much when he hasn't been trained?" they asked.

16 So Jesus told them, "My message is not my own; it comes from God who sent me. 17 Anyone who wants to do the will of God will know whether my teaching is from God or is merely my own. 18 Those who speak for themselves want glory only for themselves, but a person who seeks to honor the one who sent him speaks truth, not lies. 19 Moses gave you the law, but none of you obeys it! In fact, you are trying to kill me." (John 7:1-19 NLT).

iv. God did not allow the angry Jewish leaders and the officers they sent to seize Jesus even though they tried because His time had not yet come for his crucifixion;

- The temple guards sent by the Pharisees and Chief priests refused to seize Jesus;

    "25 Some of the people who lived in Jerusalem started to ask each other, "Isn't this the man they are trying to kill? 26 But here he is, speaking in public, and they say nothing to him. Could our leaders possibly believe that he is the Messiah?27 But how could he be? For we know where this man comes from. When the Messiah comes, he will simply appear; no one will know where he comes from."
    28 While Jesus was teaching in the Temple, he called out, "Yes, you know me, and you know where I come from. But I'm not here on my own. The one who sent me is true, and you don't know him. 29 But I know him because I come from him, and he sent me to you." 30 Then the leaders tried to arrest him; but no one laid a hand on him, because his time had not yet come. 31 Many among the crowds at the Temple believed in him. "After all," they said, "would you expect the Messiah to do more miraculous signs than this man has done?" 32 When the Pharisees heard that the crowds were whispering such things, they and the leading priests sent Temple guards to arrest Jesus. (John 7:25-32 NLT).

    40 When the crowds heard him say this, some of them declared, "Surely this man is the Prophet we've been expecting." 41 Others said, "He is the Messiah." Still others said, "But he can't

be! Will the Messiah come from Galilee?42 For the Scriptures clearly state that the Messiah will be born of the royal line of David, in Bethlehem, the village where King David was born." 43 So the crowd was divided about him. 44 Some even wanted him arrested, but no one laid a hand on him.45 When the Temple guards returned without having arrested Jesus, the leading priests and Pharisees demanded, "Why didn't you bring him in?"46 "We have never heard anyone speak like this!" the guards responded.
(John 7:40-46 NLT).

- God raised the Jewish leader Nicodemus who went in secret to question Jesus, as Jesus' defender when the leaders were rebuking the officers for not arresting him.

"45 When the Temple guards returned without having arrested Jesus, the leading priests and Pharisees demanded, "Why didn't you bring him in?"
46 "We have never heard anyone speak like this!" the guards responded.
47 "Have you been led astray, too?" the Pharisees mocked.48 "Is there a single one of us rulers or Pharisees who believes in him? 49 This foolish crowd follows him, but they are ignorant of the law. God's curse is on them!" 50 Then Nicodemus, the leader who had met with Jesus earlier, spoke up. 51 "Is it legal to convict a man before he is given a hearing?" he asked." (John 7:45-51 NLT).

- Jesus spoke boldly while teaching in the temple yet no one seized Him, again because his time to be crucified had not yet come.

"13 The Pharisees replied, "You are making those claims about yourself! Such testimony is not valid." 14 Jesus told them, "These claims are valid even though I make them about myself. For I know where I came from and where I am going, but you don't know this about me.15 You judge me by human standards, but I do not judge anyone. 16 And if I did, my judgment would be correct in every respect

because I am not alone. The Father[a] who sent me is with me. 17 Your own law says that if two people agree about something, their witness is accepted as fact. 18 I am one witness, and my Father who sent me is the other."
19 "Where is your father?" they asked. Jesus answered, "Since you don't know who I am, you don't know who my Father is. If you knew me, you would also know my Father." 20 Jesus made these statements while he was teaching in the section of the Temple known as the Treasury. But he was not arrested, because his time had not yet come. (John 8:13-20 NLT).

- When Jesus annoyed the religious leaders so much that they picked up stones to stone him, he was concealed by God and was able to leave the temple grounds unharmed.

"The people retorted, "You Samaritan devil! Didn't we say all along that you were possessed by a demon?"
49 "No," Jesus said, "I have no demon in me. For I honor my Father—and you dishonor me. 50 And though I have no wish to glorify myself, God is going to glorify me. He is the true judge. 51 I tell you the truth, anyone who obeys my teaching will never die!"
52 The people said, "Now we know you are possessed by a demon. Even Abraham and the prophets died, but you say, 'Anyone who obeys my teaching will never die!' 53 Are you greater than our father Abraham? He died, and so did the prophets. Who do you think you are?"
54 Jesus answered, "If I want glory for myself, it doesn't count. But it is my Father who will glorify me. You say, 'He is our God,' 55 but you don't even know him. I know him. If I said otherwise, I would be as great a liar as you! But I do know him and obey him. 56 Your father Abraham rejoiced as he looked forward to my coming. He saw it and was glad." 57 The people said, "You aren't even fifty years old. How can you say you have seen Abraham?" 58 Jesus answered, "I tell you the truth, before Abraham was even born, I am!" 59 At that point they picked up stones to throw

at him. But Jesus was hidden from them and left the Temple." (John 8:48-59 NLT).

3. Jesus did not accept human testimony of who he was as valid.

John was an exception because he was sent by God to testify of Jesus and his ministry. Even so, the works that Jesus did according to him are more favourable testimonies of who he was than John's testimony because they are in themselves testimonies that Father sent him.

"If I were to testify on my own behalf, my testimony would not be valid. 32 But someone else is also testifying about me, and I assure you that everything he says about me is true. 33 In fact, you sent investigators to listen to John the Baptist, and his testimony about me was true. 34 Of course, I have no need of human witnesses, but I say these things so you might be saved. 35 John was like a burning and shining lamp, and you were excited for a while about his message. 36 But I have a greater witness than John—my teachings and my miracles. The Father gave me these works to accomplish, and they prove that he sent me.37 And the Father who sent me has testified about me himself. You have never heard his voice or seen him face to face." (John 5:31-37 NLT).

Counsel ~ Encouragement

God is in control and Jesus is your prime example for Holy Living.

In the context of this chapter, as in the life of Jesus Christ:

- Nothing will happen to you that God has not allowed.

- God's plans will take place in His perfect timing, not one day early or one day late.

- God will raise people to defend you at appropriate times.

- God will protect you from your adversaries.

- You are called to entrust or commit your life to God through Christ Jesus and not to others.
    - As Jesus Christ, you are not to be preoccupied with who people say you are. Instead focus on who God says you are as His child through Christ Jesus.

- The bible says that the people of God will be known by their fruit (Matthew 7:16). If Jesus' works were the most favourable testimony as to who he was (John 5:31-37) so too should your own works or fruit (as you live in obedience to God) testify more than anything else or anyone else's testimony about you, that you belong to God.
    - In relation to fruit, the two greatest commandments are to love God and one another (Matt. 22:36-40). It is by our love for one another that people will know we are Jesus' disciples. Love is a fruit of the Spirit (Gal. 5:22-23). Expressing God's love to the brethren is the best way to witness or to testify to the world that one is a child of God.

- In Christlikeness, you are called to say and do only what the absolute will of God is and to be where only God wants you to be at any given time.

CHAPTER 5

JESUS' AUTHORITY, MISSION AND PREPARATION FOR HIS CRUCIFIXION

PART 1

JESUS' AUTHORITY AND EXPRESSIONS OF HIS NATURE THAT REVEAL HIS MISSION

I. Expressions of Jesus' nature that reveal his Mission.

In chapters 2 and 3 of this book, the "I am sayings of Jesus" in the book of John were shown to reveal his nature as God and the Son of Man and how he related to people, the following expressions of Jesus' nature reveal the same:

1. A Humble and Servable Master to His Disciples - Washer of Disciples' feet.

Jesus washes his Disciples' feet

"Before the Passover celebration, Jesus knew that his hour had come to leave this world and return to his Father. He had loved his disciples during his ministry on earth, and now he loved them to the very end.2 It was time for supper, and the devil had already prompted Judas, son of Simon Iscariot, to betray Jesus. 3 Jesus knew that the Father had given him authority over everything and that he had come from God and would return to God. 4 So he got up from the table, took off his robe, wrapped a towel around his waist, 5 and poured water into a basin. Then he began to wash the disciples' feet, drying them with the towel he had around him.

6 When Jesus came to Simon Peter, Peter said to him, "Lord, are you going to wash my feet?" 7 Jesus replied, "You don't understand now what I am doing, but someday you will."

8 "No," Peter protested, "you will never ever wash my feet!" Jesus replied, "Unless I wash you, you won't belong to me." 9 Simon Peter exclaimed, "Then wash my hands and head as well, Lord, not just my feet!" 10 Jesus replied, "A person who has bathed all over does not need to wash, except for the feet, to be entirely clean. And you disciples are clean, but not all of you." 11 For Jesus knew who would betray him. That is what he meant when he said, "Not all of you are clean." (John 13:1-11 NLT).

- **What type of disciple does Jesus, the Washer of disciples' feet seek?**

"12 After washing their feet, he put on his robe again and sat down and asked, "Do you understand what I was doing? 13 You call me 'Teacher' and 'Lord,' and you are right, because that's what I am. 14 And since I, your Lord and Teacher, have washed your feet, you ought to wash each other's feet. 15 I have given you an example to follow. Do as I have done to you. 16 I tell you the truth, slaves are not greater than their master. Nor is the messenger more important than the one who sends the message. 17 Now that you know these things, God will bless you for doing them" (John 13:12-17 NLT).

Jesus seeks a disciple who obeys his commands that they should humbly serve their fellow brethren in Christ (using washing feet as an example which he illustrated) regardless of their position in the church. If he being the Teacher and Lord of his disciples humbly washes the disciples' feet, how much more should they, including leaders among them, not wash each other's feet. The washing of feet is a revelation of selfless service which may be defined as degrading by some, however it demonstrates sacrificial and unconditional love towards a fellow human being.

2. A Zealous Worker for God.

- **Engages in works that testify of who he is**

"³⁸ But if I do his work, believe in the evidence of the miraculous works I have done, even if you don't believe me. Then you will know and understand that the Father is in me, and I am in the Father." (John 10:38NLT).

- o The Son knew who he was and who sent him on his mission.
- o Jesus did only what he saw Father doing (John 5:19),
- o gained revelation of all that Father does from Father who loves him (John 5:20),
- o could testify of himself for his testimony was valid for he
  - ▪ knew where he came from and where he was going. (John 8:12-14),
  - ▪ did works in Father's name which bears witness to Him (John 10:25),
  - ▪ has all things under his power (John 13:3).

- **Jesus' meat (nourishment or food) was to fulfil his God given mission (or works) on earth**

"…the disciples were urging Jesus, "Rabbi, eat something." 32 But Jesus replied, "I have a kind of food you know nothing about." 33 "Did someone bring him food while we were gone?" the disciples asked each other. 34 Then Jesus explained: "My nourishment comes from doing the will of God, who sent me, and from finishing his work." (John 4:31—34 NLT).

Jesus referred to doing the will of the Father (God) as meat, nourishment or food. What he was saying is that this work of God is a necessary requirement for him as eating food is for someone who is hungry. What satisfies or takes away Jesus' hunger is the "meat" or doing (activating) the will of He (God) who sent him to do and finish His work.

- **The kind of disciples Jesus seeks**

The meat Jesus "ate" (act of doing the Father's will) he taught his disciples to do the same. Anyone who is Jesus' disciple is therefore required to demonstrate the same zeal Jesus had which enabled him to fulfil the Father's will.

"You know the saying, 'Four months between planting and harvest.' But I say, wake up and look around. The fields are already ripe[a] for harvest. 36 The harvesters are paid good wages, and the fruit they harvest is people brought to eternal life. What joy awaits both the planter and the harvester alike! 37 You know the saying, 'One plants and another harvests.' And it's true. 38 I sent you to harvest where you didn't plant; others had already done the work, and now you will get to gather the harvest." (John 4:35-38 NLT).

Straight after telling his disciples that his food is to do the will of the Father, he goes on to tell the disciples (John 4:35-38) that there is an urgency for them to engage in harvesting the fields for God's sake. There are people who have been saved or become born again who need to be gathered or brought within the Body of Christ to be nurtured and cared for or discipled rather than left in "the fields" of the evil world. Anyone who is a disciple of Jesus is called to be a harvester.

This is the calling of the born again believer or disciple of Christ mentioned in Matthew 28:18-20 as follows:

"18 Jesus came and told his disciples, "I have been given all authority in heaven and on earth. 19 Therefore, go and make disciples of all the nations, baptizing them in the name of the Father and the Son and the Holy Spirit. 20 Teach these new disciples to obey all the commands I have given you. And be sure of this: I am with you always, even to the end of the age." (NLT).

II. Jesus' Authority

A. What Authority did the Father give to Jesus?

1. Resurrection/ Eternal & Abundant Life-Giver.

As the Father, Jesus is a raiser of the dead and gives the life of God to whom He chooses.
"Just as the Father gives life to those he raises from the dead, so the Son gives life to anyone he wants. And I assure you that the time is coming, indeed it's here now, when the dead will hear my voice - the voice of the Son of God. And those who listen will live. (John 5:21, 25 NLT).

" **25** Jesus told her, "I am the resurrection and the life. Anyone who believes in me will live, even after dying." (John 11:25 NLT).

Jesus is the giver of life,

- as the bread of life who makes intimacy or oneness with him possible through a two way relationship. (John 6:32-38),
- by speaking words which generate the life of God because his words are 'Spirit and Life' (John 6:63),
- as the Light of the world; to give the 'Light of life' (abundant & eternal life) to those who accept him (John 8:12),
- as the "door" or entry point for reconciliation with God; Anyone who enters him will be saved and will go in and out and "find pasture" or will never lack. (John 10:9).

"The "thief" (Satan) comes to kill, steal and destroy, but he came to give abundant and eternal life to those who accept him as Lord and Saviour (John 3:16/10:10).

2. Righteous Judge who issues the Verdict of Acquittal.

Jesus Christ is the only one who can deliver mankind from condemnation.

"²² In addition, the Father judges no one. Instead, he has given the Son absolute authority to judge, ²³ so that everyone will honor the Son, just as they honor the Father. Anyone who does not honor the Son is certainly not honoring the Father who sent him.
²⁴ "I tell you the truth, those who listen to my message and believe in God who sent me have eternal life. They will never be condemned for their sins, but they have already passed from death into life." (John 5:22-24 NLT).

This brings to mind Romans 8:1-3:
"So now there is no condemnation for those who belong to Christ Jesus. 2 And because you belong to him, the power of the life-giving Spirit has freed you from the power of sin that leads to death. 3 The Law of Moses was unable to save us because of the weakness of our sinful nature. So God did what the law could not do. He sent his own Son in a body like the bodies we sinners have. And in that body God declared an end to sin's control over us by giving his Son as a sacrifice for our sins." (NLT).

A man cannot in himself give a verdict of condemnation to another because there is no man without sin.

"Jesus returned to the Mount of Olives, ² but early the next morning he was back again at the Temple. A crowd soon gathered, and he sat down and taught them. ³ As he was speaking, the teachers of religious law and the Pharisees brought a woman who had been caught in the act of adultery. They put her in front of the crowd.⁴ "Teacher," they said to Jesus, "this woman was caught in the act of adultery. ⁵ The Law of Moses says to stone her. What do you say?"

⁶ They were trying to trap him into saying something they could use against him, but Jesus stooped down and wrote in the dust with his finger. ⁷ They kept demanding an answer, so he stood up again and said, "All right, but let the one who has never sinned throw the first stone!" ⁸ Then he stooped down again and wrote in the dust.

⁹ When the accusers heard this, they slipped away one by one, beginning with the oldest, until only Jesus was left in the middle of the crowd with the woman. ¹⁰ Then Jesus stood up again and said to the woman, "Where are your accusers? Didn't even one of them condemn you?" ¹¹ "No, Lord," she said. And Jesus said, "Neither do I. Go and sin no more." (John 8:1-11 NLT).

3. He is a Righteous Judge.

All Judgement has been entrusted to the Son by the Father.
"The Father doesn't judge anyone. He has entrusted judgment entirely to the Son" (John 5:22 NLT).
His judgement is true or valid because He is not alone in making judgement, he does it with the Father who sent Him (John 8:15-16).
The testimony of two witnesses is valid according to the Law of Moses., likewise he bears witness of himself and the Father who sent him also bears witness of him (John 8:18).

4. Care-Giver or Shepherd.

Jesus is the Good Shepherd who cares for the sheep and gives his life for them. (John 10:12-13, 15-18).

Jesus is the Good Shepherd who is identifiable by his sheep. (John 10:2-5). As the Good Shepherd, Jesus is one who

- gives security, protection and assurance to those who are his sheep
  (John 10:24-30).

- gathers other sheep (unsaved) not yet of the fold and brings them into the fold so as to be the Shepherd of all (John 10:16).

- gives life abundantly unlike the thief who comes (not by the Door but another way John 10:1) to kill steal, and destroy (John 10:10).

5. Teacher

Jesus teaches by supernatural revelation from God.

When people marvelled or were amazed by Jesus' teaching even though he had not studied, He replied that His teaching was given by "Him who sent me", meaning God the Father" (John 7:14-18).

6. Healer

Jesus healed on any day including the Sabbath despite opposition from those who abide by the Law of Moses which stipulates that no work should be done on the Sabbath. To the law abiders (Jews and their religious leaders who did not believe in Jesus), work included healing on the Sabbath (John 5 & 9). But Jesus came to perfect the Law by teaching people the correct manner of interpreting the law so as to give glory to God. Healing on the Sabbath as taught and demonstrated by Jesus was not breaking the Law.

7. A Rabbi with Authority over Nature & Elements.

Jesus calmed the strong winds and rough waters (John 6:16-21).

B. In what manner did Jesus demonstrate the Father's Authority?

1. He was constantly at work; working as the Father was working.

"[16] So the Jewish leaders began harassing Jesus for breaking the Sabbath rules. [17] But Jesus replied, "My Father is always working, and so am I." (John 5:16-17 NLT).

2. He did only what he saw the Father doing and what he gained revelation from the Father to do.

"¹⁹ So Jesus explained, "I tell you the truth, the Son can do nothing by himself. He does only what he sees the Father doing. Whatever the Father does, the Son also does. ²⁰ For the Father loves the Son and shows him everything he is doing. In fact, the Father will show him how to do even greater works than healing this man. Then you will truly be astonished... ²⁴ "I tell you the truth, those who listen to my message and believe in God who sent me have eternal life. They will never be condemned for their sins, but they have already passed from death into life." (John 5:19-20, 24 NLT).

3. He did the works that the Father gave him to do which bore witness to the fact that the Father sent him.

Jesus' works testify that the Father sent him.

"36 But I have a greater witness than John—my teachings and my miracles. The Father gave me these works to accomplish, and they prove that he sent me. 37 And the Father who sent me has testified about me himself. You have never heard his voice or seen him face to face." (John 5:36-37 NLT).

When masses doubted Jesus (John 7:25-27), this was what "he called out, "Yes, you know me, and you know where I come from. But I'm not here on my own. The one who sent me is true, and you don't know him. (John 7:28NLT).

4. He reproduced after himself in the life of those given to him by the Father.

Jesus' authority can only be accepted and therefore exercised by those who come to Him because a way is made for them to do so by the Father.

"Then what will you think if you see the Son of Man ascend to heaven again? 63 The Spirit alone gives eternal life. Human effort accomplishes nothing. And the very words I have spoken to you are spirit and life. 64 But some of you do not believe me." (For Jesus knew from the beginning which ones didn't believe, and he knew who would betray him.) 65 Then he said, "That is why I said that people can't come to me unless the Father gives them to me." (John 6:62-65 NLT).

JESUS AND HIS DISCIPLES: PREPARING FOR HIS CRUCIFIXION.

PART 1

1. Jesus was willing to suffer mockery, shame, beatings and crucifixion to fulfil Father's mission.

Though Satan had no part in him (John 14:30) and Christ Jesus had no sin (2 Corinthians 5:21), he accepted to die because his love for the Father compelled him to be obedient to Him.

"I don't have much more time to talk to you, because the ruler of this world approaches. He has no power over me." (John 14:30NLT).

"a. My Father! If it is possible, let this cup of suffering be taken away from me. b. Yet I want your will to be done, not mine." (Matthew 26:39NLT).

It appears from Jesus' words in Matthew 26:39a (above) during his prayers in the garden of Gethsemane that he would have preferred not to have gone through with his death.

An ordinary human being would have said "LORD is there not any other way that man can be redeemed than me having to go through this?", Jesus' words implied he was saying the same thing or words to that effect. As the Son of Man, so as to identify with mankind, it is understandable that he would have such emotions at such a time when he was under immense spiritual pressure when Satan and his hordes had the permission from God to cause his suffering and death. Jesus however had no intention of disobeying Father God.

"…Yet I want your will to be done, not mine." (Matthew 26:39b NLT). This is because he was God and anointed to go through the ordeal of suffering immensely unto death.

2. Jesus Christ, though persecuted was fearless & bold before his persecutors.

As expressed by the Apostle John, people were afraid of confessing that Jesus was the Christ; a miracle worker or healer (see point 2. below). They were afraid that they would be barred from entering the synagogue if they were in anyway seen to be followers of Jesus.

If his disciples were not allowed into the synagogues or temples, then it is obvious that Jesus was also not welcomed or he was barred from these places. However Jesus still boldly entered such places and preached in them as well whether the unbelieving Jews and their leaders wanted him to or not.

Jesus came to do the will of Him (Abba Father) who sent him and would not let anyone deter him from that. He boldly preached, taught and healed in religious gatherings including feasts. He was also fearless of the religious leaders when he

-exercised his authority by confronting and rebuking the
traders in the temple (Matthew 21:10-14).

-read some of Isaiah 61 in the synagogue and spoke in
such a way as to make those gathered understand that he was the one about whom it referred.

"The Spirit of the LORD is upon me, for he has anointed me to bring Good News to the poor. He has sent me to proclaim that captives will be released, that the blind will see, that the oppressed will be set free and that the time of the LORD's favour has come" (Luke 4:18 NLT).

The unbelieving religious leaders tried to arrest him a number of times but were unable to because God's appointed time for his death had not come.

When Jesus was finally arrested and he was questioned as to who he was, he told them the truth as to who he was.

"Now Jesus was standing before Pilate, the Roman governor, "Are you the king of the Jews?" the governor asked him. Jesus replied, "You have said it". But when the leading priests and the elders made their accusations against him, Jesus remained silent. "Don't you hear all these charges they are brining against you?" Pilate demanded. But Jesus made no response to any of the charges, much to the governor's surprise."(Matthew 27:11-14 NLT).

3. **Jesus knew and so kept to the timing of God in relation to his arrest and crucifixion.**

Jesus is shown to resist being seized or arrested and so killed prematurely (before his time) by his enemies as well as being forcefully made a king by his followers; he would slip away and refrain from going to certain places at certain times. Also God prevented Jesus' accusers from succeeding in stoning him or capturing him prematurely.

But when the appointed time came for his betrayal, arrest and death at the Passover meal, Jesus himself gave the go ahead for Satan through Judas one of his disciples to betray him.

4. **When the time came for his death, Jesus prepared his disciples in the final hour. He did so by teaching them and highlighting the consequences of being his disciples.**

A. Jesus taught his disciples the importance of

- Loving one another as he loved them: Jesus gave them a new commandment
  "So now I am giving you a new commandment: Love each other. Just as I have loved you, you should love each other" (John 13:34 NLT).

  Love confessed must be demonstrated, and Jesus gave an example as to how this love can be demonstrated when he washed his disciples' feet, even the one who would later betray him, Judas Iscariot (John 13:5-14).

- Loving Him demonstrated through obeying him just as he loves Father and obeys Him. (John 14:21-26).

- Knowing that his physical absence did not mean he was rejecting them, or that they were orphans, rather it was necessary that he dies and resurrects so that
  - He goes to Father to prepare a place for them in Father's heavenly realm and promises to come for them (John 14:1-4).
  - He sends the Holy Spirit, the Spirit of Truth, who testifies of Jesus and reminds the disciples of his teachings and prevents Jesus disciples from having the orphan (abandonment, rejection) spirit following Jesus ascension.

- Instituting the Lord's Supper in remembrance of him until he comes;
  - breaking bread representing his body broken for them in his suffering and crucifixion
  - drinking wine representing his blood shed for them when he was crucified.

Jesus spoke about the importance of his flesh and blood:
"52 Then the people began arguing with each other about what he meant. "How can this man give us his flesh to eat?" they asked. 53 So Jesus said again, "I tell you the truth, unless you eat the flesh of the Son of Man and drink his blood, you cannot have eternal life within you. 54 But anyone who eats my flesh and drinks my blood has eternal life, and I will raise that person at the last day. 55 For my flesh is true food, and my blood is true drink. 56 Anyone who eats my flesh and drinks my blood remains in me, and I in him. 57 I live because of the living Father who sent me; in the same way, anyone who feeds on me will live because of me. 58 I am the true bread that came down from heaven. Anyone who eats this bread will not die as your ancestors did (even though they ate the manna) but will live forever." 59 He said these things while he was teaching in the synagogue in Capernaum." (John 6:52-59 NLT).

The Apostle Luke gives the account of Christ Jesus at the Passover meal with his disciples telling them to partake of the Passover Meal (what is today called "Lord's Supper") in remembrance of him as follows:

"He took some bread and gave thanks to God for it. Then he broke it in pieces and gave it to the disciples, saying, "This is my body, which is given for you. Do this in remembrance of me. After supper he took another cup of wine and said "This cup is the new covenant between God and his people-an agreement confirmed with my blood, which is poured out as a sacrifice for you." (Luke 22:19-20 NLT).

B. Jesus highlighted the consequences of being his disciples, during his ministry and after his death:

I. THE PERSECUTION OF JESUS' DISCIPLES DURING AND AFTER HIS MINISTRY.

Before his death, Jesus told his disciples that they will be persecuted by being put out of the synagogues and those who kill them will think they are doing God a favour. The persecutors acted in that manner because they do not know the Father nor Jesus. During Jesus' ministry it is clear that the unbelieving Jews and religious leaders had agreed that anyone who confessed that Jesus was the Messiah would be put out of the synagogue. This was confirmed in this account of the man who received his sight after Jesus spat on clay and put it over his eyes and told him to go and wash in the pool of Siloam:

"The Jewish leaders still refused to believe the man had been blind and could now see, so they called in his parents. 19 They asked them, "Is this your son? Was he born blind? If so, how can he now see?" 20 His parents replied, "We know this is our son and that he was born blind, 21 but we don't know how he can see or who healed him. Ask him. He is old enough to speak for himself." 22 His parents said this because they were afraid of the Jewish leaders, who had announced that anyone saying Jesus was the Messiah would be expelled from the synagogue.23 That's why they said, "He is old enough. Ask him." (John 9:18-23 NLT).

Not long before his betrayal and death, Jesus highlighted the consequences of being his disciples:

1. FEAR CAUSED JESUS' DISCIPLES TO DESERT OR DENY HIM.

Speaking to his disciples, Jesus said that they will desert him. Peter thought he would not fall away nor desert Jesus. Jesus however told Peter that he would deny him before the cock crows three times. Such actions on the part of the disciples were motivated by fear of Jesus' accusers.

Three slightly different versions of the account are revealed by different Apostles as follows:
"Then Jesus said to them, "You will all fall away because of Me this night, for it is written, 'I WILL STRIKE DOWN THE SHEPHERD, AND THE SHEEP OF THE FLOCK SHALL BE SCATTERED.' 32 "But after I have been raised, I will go ahead of you to Galilee." 33 But Peter said to Him, "Even though all may fall away because of You, I will never fall away."34 Jesus said to

him, "Truly I say to you that this very night, before a rooster crows, you will deny Me three times." 35 Peter said to Him, "Even if I have to die with You, I will not deny You." All the disciples said the same thing too." (Matthew 26:31-35 NLT) (identical to Mark's account)

"Simon, Simon, behold, Satan has demanded *permission* to sift you like wheat;**32** but I have prayed for you, that your faith may not fail; and you, when once you have turned again, strengthen your brothers." **33** But he said to Him, "Lord, with You I am ready to go both to prison and to death!" **34** And He said, "I say to you, Peter, the rooster will not crow today until you have denied three times that you know Me." (Luke 22:31-34 NLT).

31 As soon as Judas left the room, Jesus said, "The time has come for the Son of Man to enter into his glory, and God will be glorified because of him. **32** And since God receives glory because of the Son, he will give his own glory to the Son, and he will do so at once. **33** Dear children, I will be with you only a little longer. And as I told the Jewish leaders, you will search for me, but you can't come where I am going.

34 So now I am giving you a new commandment: Love each other. Just as I have loved you, you should love each other. **35** Your love for one another will prove to the world that you are my disciples." **36** Simon Peter asked, "Lord, where are you going?" And Jesus replied, "You can't go with me now, but you will follow me later." **37** "But why can't I come now, Lord?" he asked. "I'm ready to die for you." **38** Jesus answered, "Die for me? I tell you the truth, Peter—before the rooster crows tomorrow morning, you will deny three times that you even know me.(John 13:31-38NLT).

2. HATRED FROM THE WORLD.

The world would hate Jesus' disciples because it hated him, their master for as Jesus said "a servant is not greater than his master" (John 15:18/John 17:14).

3. TROUBLE IN THE WORLD.

They will have trouble in the world, but they must "be of good cheer" or rejoice for he has overcome the world and so through him they will also overcome the World (John 16:33).

Many years later, the Apostle Paul reminded the Christians in Rome that they were overcomers through Christ who loves them (Romans 8:37).

II. JESUS' DEATH WAS FOR THE GLORY OF GOD.

Introduction
What is the meaning of Glory and Glorify?
Oxford advanced Learner's Dictionary
Noun: Glory
- High renown or honour won by notable achievements.
- Magnificence or great beauty
- Praise, worship and thanksgiving offered to a deity.

Merriam-Webster dictionary to glorify:
Transitive verb: Glorify
- To make glorious by bestowing honor, praise or admiration
- To light up brilliantly.

Believers in Jesus give glory to him when they

1. Fellowship with God;
   -Moses' face shone with the glory of God when he had face to face fellowship with God.
   "²⁹ When Moses came down Mount Sinai carrying the two stone tablets inscribed with the terms of the covenant, he wasn't aware that his face had become radiant because he had spoken to the LORD." (Exodus 34:29 NLT).

¹¹ Inside the Tent of Meeting, the LORD would speak to Moses face to face, as one speaks to a friend. Afterward Moses would return to the camp, but the young man who assisted him, Joshua son of Nun, would remain behind in the Tent of Meeting. (Exodus 33:11 NLT).

-Obey Jesus' commands

21 Those who accept my commandments and obey them are the ones who love me. And because they love me, my Father will love them. And I will love them and reveal myself to each of them." 22 Judas (not Judas Iscariot, but the other disciple with that name) said to him, "Lord, why are you going to reveal yourself only to us and not to the world at large?" 23 Jesus replied, "All who love me will do what I say. My Father will love them, and we will come and make our home with each of them. 24 Anyone who doesn't love me will not obey me. And remember, my words are not my own. What I am telling you is from the Father who sent me. 25 I am telling you these things now while I am still with you. 26 But when the Father sends the Advocate as my representative—that is, the Holy Spirit—he will teach you everything and will remind you of everything I have told you. (John 14:21-26 NLT)

2. Worship God
   All the nations you made; will come and bow before you, Lord; they will praise your holy name. (Psalm 86:9 NLT)

   ¹⁴ The priests could not continue their service because of the cloud, for the glorious presence of the LORD filled the Temple of God. (2 Chronicles 5:14 NLT)

3. Do all things as unto the LORD
   Believers in Jesus are required to glorify God and Christ in all they do by doing everything as if it were unto them. (Corinthians 10:31)
4. All heaven declares His glory: (Psalm 19:1)

5. Angels glorify God: (Isaiah 6:1-3)

HOW DID JESUS GLORIFY THE FATHER IN HIS DEATH?

Having glorified the Father in his ministry, when the time came for his death, Jesus looked up to heaven and said, "Father, the hour has come. Glorify your Son so he can give glory back to you. (John 17:1NLT). Jesus accepted to glorify the Father by agreeing to undergo the process of death, burial and resurrection which was the Father's will for him. Jesus, the Son referred to his pending death as something which was to glorify him. He also acknowledged that Father is ultimately glorified through his glorification.

Thus the humiliation, suffering and crucifixion of Jesus Christ by religious leaders of the nation of Israel was for Jesus' glorification as well as that of Father's through him. As a result of Jesus' ordeal, he and God revealed themselves to be exalted and magnified as sovereign over the whole universe and the only ones capable of delivering mankind from sin, sickness, disease, demonic possession and control.

C. Jesus told his disciples why he was speaking to them the way he was prior to his betrayal.

"I have told you these things before they happen so that when they do happen, you will believe." (John 14: 29 NLT).
" I have told you these things so that you will be filled with my joy. Yes, your joy will overflow!" (John 15:11NLT)."I have told you all this so that you may have peace in me. Here on earth you will have many trials and sorrows. But take heart, because I have overcome the world." (John 16:33NLT).

PART 2

JESUS' DISCUSSIONS WITH HIS DISCIPLES CLOSE TO THE TIME OF HIS CRUCIFIXION

1. GOD'S APPOINTED TIME FOR JESUS TO BE BETRAYED AND TO BE SEIZED BY RELIGIOUS LEADERS FOR HIS CRUCIFIXION.

The Passover meal "Last Supper" took place before the washing of the feet of Jesus (John 13:2-5, 18-30). Jesus' disciples were commanded to do both. What happened at the "Last Supper"?

The time had come for Jesus' betrayal and the one who became his disciple but had been marked by God to be the betrayer was provoked to do so by Jesus at this appointed time. It was at this last Passover feast before his crucifixion that Jesus spoke of which of his disciples would betray him. He pointed the disciple out by the act of dipping bread into wine and offering it to that disciple (Judas) telling him to go and do what he was meant to do (John 13:21-32).

JUDAS – UNDER THE GOVERNANCE OF SATAN THE FATHER OF LIES, KILLER, STEALER AND DESTROYER.

Judas was one of Jesus' twelve disciples yet he was insincere. He was consciously in sin; Judas' nature was already apparent as a deceiver because as a keeper of the disciples' money bag, he used to steal money from it. He even voiced out in protest when Mary, the sister of Martha and Lazarus washed Jesus' feet with expensive perfume, saying that the perfume could have been sold and the money given to the poor (John 12 Judas was more concerned with the monetary value of the perfume and saw the act of using it on

Jesus' feet as wastage. Therefore in Judas' opinion, Jesus was not worthy enough to merit such expensive perfume being poured on his feet. This exposes Judas' heart condition; he did not love, value or respect Jesus in the way that one would expect a disciple to do so.

Judas was therefore imitating his father Satan, the one Jesus said

> - came to kill steal and destroy unlike him (Jesus) who came to give abundant life
> (John 10:10).
> - is a liar, he has been lying from the beginning and was the father of the unbelieving Jewish leaders because they refused to believe his words including the fact that Father God sent him.

"Instead, you are trying to kill me because I told you the truth, which I heard from God. Abraham never did such a thing. [41] No, you are imitating your real father." They replied, "We aren't illegitimate children! God himself is our true Father." [42] Jesus told them, "If God were your Father, you would love me, because I have come to you from God. I am not here on my own, but he sent me. [43] Why can't you understand what I am saying? It's because you can't even hear me! [44] For you are the children of your father the devil, and you love to do the evil things he does. He was a murderer from the beginning. He has always hated the truth, because there is no truth in him. When he lies, it is consistent with his character; for he is a liar and the father of lies. [45] So when I tell the truth, you just naturally don't believe me! [46] Which of you can truthfully accuse me of sin? And since I am telling you the truth, why don't you believe me? [47] Anyone who belongs to God listens gladly to the words of God. But you don't listen because you don't belong to God." (John 8:40-47 NLT).

2. A NEW COMMANDMENT WAS GIVEN TO JESUS' DISCIPLES.

"So now I am giving you a new commandment: Love each other.

Just as I have loved you, you should love each other.³⁵ Your love for one another will prove to the world that you are my disciples." (John 13:34-35 NLT).

3. THE DISTINCTION BETWEEN THE DESTINY OF JESUS' DISCIPLES AND UNBELIEVING JEWS.

The disciples of Jesus are the only ones who, having believed in him and travailed for his sake, will in due course have access to where he is going after his death, burial and resurrection (John 13:36, John 14), which is his return to Father God.
Jesus' pre-death promises to His disciples according to John 14, was that

- He was going to Father to prepare a place "mansion" for them individually (vs 1-2).
- He would come again and take them to where he is (vs 3).
- They knew where he was going (vs 4) and the way to get there which is
    - through him, for he is the way, truth and life. And that no man can go to the Father except through him (vs 6).
- Knowing and seeing Jesus is equivalent to knowing and seeing Father (vs 7-9).
    - He asked his disciples to believe
        - in him also as they believe in the God of Israel
        - that the Father is in him and he is in the Father.
        - that his words are not his own but that of the Father dwelling in him who is working through him (vs 14:10).
        - in him because of his works (vs 11).

- Anyone who believes in him, the works that he does, they will also be able to do and even greater works than he did after he returns to the Father (vs 12).
- The result of believing in him and doing his works/greater works is that whatever that person asks for in his name, he will do it. Prayers being answered by Jesus is for the sake of the Father being glorified in the Son (vs 13).
- He will do whatever his disciples ask in his name (vs 14).
- If his disciples love him and keep his commandments, then he will pray to Father God who will send a comforter to them in Jesus absence, who will abide with them forever (vs 16-17).

Encouragement

Christ's Delegated Authority & Suffering

When you exercise your authority as Christ you make an impact in the world and in the lives of multitudes.

If you are a believer in Jesus Christ, devoted to God through the Word (Bible) and Holy Spirit, then exercising your authority delegated to you by Christ Jesus means you

- o glorify God and His Kingdom.

- o are empowered by the Holy Spirit and commissioned to preach, disciple and be a baptizer in the name of the Father, Son and the Holy Spirit. You are also commissioned to heal the sick and cast out demons (Matthew 28:18-20/Mark 16:17-18).

"My Father! If it is possible, let this cup of suffering be taken away from me. Yet I want your will to be done, not mine." (Matthew 26:39NLT).

These words of Jesus should remind every believer in him who feels compelled to complain or give up when they are suffering affliction that their pain and suffering is never a permanent condition or situation because Jesus also went through pain, suffering and death for the sake of man. No affliction man goes through will ever be worse than what Jesus went through. Jesus' love for the Father compelled him to accept His will that Jesus should die for the sake of mankind's redemption.

So instead of complaining or giving up, a believer in Christ should rejoice because Jesus has gone through every emotion of pain and suffering on our behalf. We must also trust God to be with us in our afflictions as we pray and take comfort in God's Word. God's plan is to work all things out for the good of those who love Him (Romans 8:28).

The washing of the disciple's feet by Jesus and his treatment of them as intimate friends:

This is supposed to speak to leaders in Christian ministry that

- they need not be insecure in their position of delegated authority and power because it is a calling and gift of God through Christ Jesus; They should therefore not be afraid to demonstrate Christ's love to their congregation members in selfless ways as Christ demonstrated to his disciples by washing their feet.
  Those Jesus ministered the will of the Father to, he called friends (John 15:15-18) and drew them close. Jesus was teaching by example with expressions of selfless, unconditional love in his interpersonal

relationships. It is possible to be a leader and at the same time a close friend of those one is leading.

CHAPTER 6

TRUE DISCIPLES OF JESUS CHRIST ARE LEGITIMATE CHILDREN OF GOD

PART 1

THE LEGITIMATE CHILDREN OF GOD IN A NEW COVENANT CONTEXT.

I. LEGITIMATE CHILDREN OF GOD ARE DEFINED IN THE OLD TESTAMENT ERA OF "TEMPORARY TYPES AWAITING THE PERMANENT REALITY":

THEY ARE ETHNIC ISRAELITES AND GENTILES WHO ACCEPT THE GOD OF ISRAEL.

1. ETHNIC ISRAELITES.
The lives of the Israelites, descendants of Abraham, Isaac and Jacob were governed by the Law of Moses (Ceremonial Laws and Moral Law -Ten Commandments) which was a "temporary type" prior to God's appointed time to send the "Permanent Reality" who is Jesus Christ.

2. GENTILES WHO ACCEPT THE GOD OF ISRAEL AS THEIR GOD.
Anyone, a foreigner or slave who was not an Israelite by ethnicity but accepted the God of Israel (who is also creator God) was graciously declared by God as His covenanted child.

A clear affirmation of this was spoken by God as follows through the Prophet Isaiah:

Chapter 56
This is what the LORD says:

"Be just and fair to all.
   Do what is right and good,
for I am coming soon to rescue you
   and to display my righteousness among you.
² Blessed are all those
   who are careful to do this.
Blessed are those who honor my Sabbath days of rest
   and keep themselves from doing wrong.
³ "Don't let foreigners who commit themselves to the LORD say,
   'The LORD will never let me be part of his people.'
And don't let the eunuchs say,
   'I'm a dried-up tree with no children and no future.'
⁴ For this is what the LORD says:
I will bless those eunuchs
   who keep my Sabbath days holy
and who choose to do what pleases me
   and commit their lives to me.
⁵ I will give them—within the walls of my house—
   a memorial and a name
   far greater than sons and daughters could give.
For the name I give them is an everlasting one.
   It will never disappear!
⁶ "I will also bless the foreigners who commit themselves to the LORD,
   who serve him and love his name,
who worship him and do not desecrate the Sabbath day of rest,
   and who hold fast to my covenant.
⁷ I will bring them to my holy mountain of Jerusalem
   and will fill them with joy in my house of prayer.
I will accept their burnt offerings and sacrifices,
   because my Temple will be called a house of prayer for all nations.
⁸ For the Sovereign LORD,
   who brings back the outcasts of Israel, says:
I will bring others, too,
   besides my people Israel." (Isaiah 56:1-8 NLT).

II. LEGITIMATE CHILDREN OF GOD ARE DEFINED IN THE NEW TESTAMENT ERA OF JESUS CHRIST (THE "PERMANENT REALITY"):

THEY ARE DISCIPLES OF JESUS CHRIST.

A. GOD SENT JESUS CHRIST TO BE THE MEANS THROUGH WHOM MAN IS SAVED OR BORN AGAIN

In God's appointed time, he sent Jesus Christ "Permanent Reality", The only Way (John 14:6) for man to be reconciled to God the Father.

Jesus replaced the Ceremonial Laws/Rituals of the Mosaic Law
God wanted man to have a means to make peace with Him and sent Jesus Christ as a mediator or advocate on behalf of man. In fact God came in the flesh, in the person of Jesus Christ (2 Corinthians 5:19) to make this possible. God's reason for doing so was because He loved the world so much and offered mankind a means of redemption through Jesus Christ. This is so that whosoever believes in him will not perish but have eternal life (John 3:16)

Jesus assumed this position through the shedding of his blood as the sacrificial lamb when he died on the cross and also assumed the position of the High Priest. In this way Jesus, the Permanent reality, replaced the animal sacrifice and High Priest of Israel's ceremonial laws/regulations – "temporary types") who made atonement for man's sins once and for all. As a result the yearly sacrifices of Israel by the High Priest, a temporary type, was no longer necessary.

Jesus perfected the Law:
He interpreted it in the new covenant context.

[17] "Don't misunderstand why I have come. I did not come to abolish the law of Moses or the writings of the prophets. No, I came to accomplish their purpose. [18] I tell you the truth, until heaven and earth disappear, not even the smallest detail of God's

law will disappear until its purpose is achieved. **19** So if you ignore the least commandment and teach others to do the same, you will be called the least in the Kingdom of Heaven. But anyone who obeys God's laws and teaches them will be called great in the Kingdom of Heaven. (Matthew 5:17-19 NLT). The Sermon on the Mount gives further revelation as to how Jesus came to perfect the Law of Moses (Matthew 5-7)

ONE MUST BE SAVED TO BE A CHILD OF GOD, A CITIZEN OF HIS KINGDOM

When a man accepts Jesus Christ as Lord and Saviour, then it means he is saved from sin and has been reconciled to God. These verses explain clearly how and when this happens:

"9 If you openly declare that Jesus is Lord and believe in your heart that God raised him from the dead, you will be saved.10 For it is by believing in your heart that you are made right with God, and it is by openly declaring your faith that you are saved. (Romans 10:9-10 NLT).

"YOU MUST BE BORN AGAIN" IS ANOTHER WAY OF SAYING "YOU MUST BE SAVED"

When Jesus said to Nicodemus "I tell you the truth, unless you are born again, you cannot see the Kingdom of God." (John 3:3NLT) he was actually saying that he must be saved to enter the Kingdom of God, but expressing it in a different way.

"There was a man named Nicodemus, a Jewish religious leader who was a Pharisee. **2** After dark one evening, he came to speak with Jesus. "Rabbi," he said, "we all know that God has sent you to teach us. Your miraculous signs are evidence that God is with you."
3 Jesus replied, "I tell you the truth, unless you are born again, you cannot see the Kingdom of God." **4** "What do you mean?" exclaimed Nicodemus. "How can an old man go back into his mother's womb and be born again?"

⁵ Jesus replied, "I assure you, no one can enter the Kingdom of God without being born of water and the Spirit. ⁶ Humans can reproduce only human life, but the Holy Spirit gives birth to spiritual life.⁷ So don't be surprised when I say, 'You must be born again.' ⁸ The wind blows wherever it wants. Just as you can hear the wind but can't tell where it comes from or where it is going, so you can't explain how people are born of the Spirit." (John 3:1-8NLT).

When a person is naturally born, he or she is spiritually dead because they inherited the generational innate sinful nature of Adam and Eve that they and their offspring acquired after they chose to disobey God in the garden of Eden. But when one accepts Jesus Christ as their Lord and Saviour, a miracle happens in which Jesus Christ comes and lives within them.

¹⁷ This means that anyone who belongs to Christ has become a new person. The old life is gone; a new life has begun! (2 Corinthians 5:17NLT)

THE IMPORTANCE OF THE HOLY SPIRIT AND WATER IN THE BORN AGAIN EXPERIENCE

1. HOLY SPIRIT

The Holy Spirit is a witness to the fact that the individual has Christ living within them, for the Holy Spirit is the testimony of Jesus (John 15:26-27) and bears witness with their spirits that they are children of God (Romans 8:15).

"⁹ But you are not controlled by your sinful nature. You are controlled by the Spirit if you have the Spirit of God living in you. (And remember that those who do not have the Spirit of Christ living in them do not belong to him at all." (Romans 8:9NLT).

¹¹ The Spirit of God, who raised Jesus from the dead, lives in you. And just as God raised Christ Jesus from the dead, he will give life to your mortal bodies by this same Spirit living within you. (Romans 8:11 NLT)

The Holy Spirit indwelling the believer is a sign that they are spiritually alive because they have accepted Jesus Christ as Lord and Saviour. In other words they are re-born spiritually; No longer dead but alive in Christ, they are therefore born again; They have the life of God in their present lives and the promise of eternal life. Being born again spiritually is a mystery of God that cannot be adequately expressed in words (John3:8).

These verses express being born again:
"Some of us are Jews, some are Gentiles, some are slaves, and some are free. But we have all been baptized into one body by one Spirit, and we all share the same Spirit. (1 Corinth. 12:13NLT).

BAPTISM IN THE HOLY SPIRIT

Having been saved or united with Christ as part of the church which also involves the Holy Spirit as mentioned earlier, it is then necessary and important for the disciple of Jesus to receive the Baptism in the Holy Spirit. The Baptism in the Holy Spirit is a supernatural outpouring of the Spirit of God upon a born again believer in Jesus Christ to prepare them for effective or powerful ministry in the world at large.

When Jesus resurrected from the dead and met with his disciples, he told them not to depart from Jerusalem but to wait for the promise of the Holy Spirit (Act 1:4-5).

John the Baptist had said "[16] John answered their questions by saying, "I baptize you with water; but someone is coming soon who is greater than I am—so much greater that I'm not even worthy to be his slave and untie the straps of his sandals. He will baptize you with the Holy Spirit and with fire." (Luke 3:16NLT).

As John the Baptist immersed or drenched people in water, Jesus would immerse or drench his disciples with the Holy Spirit so to speak.

This happened on the Day of Pentecost and has been happening since;

"On the day of Pentecost all the believers were meeting together in one place. ² Suddenly, there was a sound from heaven like the roaring of a mighty windstorm, and it filled the house where they were sitting.³ Then, what looked like flames or tongues of fire appeared and settled on each of them. ⁴ And everyone present was filled with the Holy Spirit and began speaking in other languages,[b] as the Holy Spirit gave them this ability. (Acts 2:1-4NLT)

Speaking in tongues is evidence that Baptism in the Holy Spirit has taken place.

2. WATER

The act of water baptism is necessary and important because it affirms one has died with
Christ (the act of descending in the water) and resurrected (the act of coming up from the water) with him in newness. Jesus Christ was baptised before he started his public ministry and it was during his baptism that the Spirit of God descended upon him and God spoke openly about who Jesus was:

"After his baptism, as Jesus came up out of the water, the heavens were opened and he saw the Spirit of God descending like a dove and settling on him. ¹⁷ And a voice from heaven said, "This is my dearly loved Son, who brings me great joy." (Matthew 3:16-17NLT).

Jesus Christ the Messiah of the World – redefined the meaning of legitimate child of God in the old covenant context.

When Jesus Christ came into the world, sent by God through the line of Judah (who was the son of Jacob, Abraham's son) in the nation of Israel, there was a redefinition of who a legitimate child of God is based on the New Covenant according to Jeremiah 31:31-34, fulfilled by Jesus Christ.

"There is salvation in no one else! God has given no other name under heaven by which we must be saved."(Acts 4:12 NLT).

Since Jesus came, the following can only be legitimate children of God if they are born again (John 3) or saved by accepting Jesus Christ as their Lord and Saviour through confession and believing in their hearts (Romans 10:9-10) that he is the Messiah:

a) Gentiles among the nations who
   - do not worship the creator God who is also the God of Israel, but worship a god or several gods of man's making, often times through idols or images.
   - may not worship a god or gods directly or through images and idols, but are self-reliant and self-dependant. Some may call themselves atheists and others satanists.
   - for spiritual enlightenment and perfection they meditate on words of wisdom of religious sages or philosophers of the world some of whom are leaders of cults or ungodly religions, often times using idols or images of them during worship.

b) Israelites (collectively called "Jews" by some people); by ethnicity, descendants of Abraham, Isaac and Jacob. The promise of salvation of all of them is assured by God (see Romans Chapters 10 and 11).

c) Gentiles who assume the title of Jew for these reasons: While they are not ethnic Israelites (descendants of Abraham, Isaac and Jacob) their ancestors became covenanted children of God because of their acceptance of the God of Israel as their LORD (Isaiah 56).
   They include those whose ancestors converted to Judaism centuries ago in ancient and modern times, multitudes of whom assumed the name "Jews" so that several of their descendants even identify as ethnic Israelites although they are not.

B. THE NEW COVENANT DEFINES WHO A TRUE LEGITIMATE CHILD OF FATHER GOD IS:

Scripture: John Chapter 8

Jesus Christ distinguishes between God's (Father of truth's) children and Satan's ("Father of lies'") children. This is because the fate of the sinful is to die an eternal death (John 8:21-24).

Some Jews believed in him while others did not. Those who did not believe in him were angry with him because he said God was his Father and he taught them that being descendants of Abraham (John 8:30-47) did not automatically make them righteous for whoever commits sin is "the servant of sin" and satan is the father of the sinful regardless of their ethnicity or nationality.

1. **Who are true children of Abraham or Children of God the Father? Not those by ancestral descent from Abraham, but those who love and believe in Jesus Christ (who is God in the flesh "Son of Man" vs 28, therefore existed before Abraham. Jesus said "before Abraham was, I am" vs 58) and his teachings which he received from Father God (Father of truth), which is the truth and therefore capable of setting people free.**

John 8:12-42, 48-59:
"¹² Jesus spoke to the people once more and said, "I am the light of the world. If you follow me, you won't have to walk in darkness, because you will have the light that leads to life." ¹³ The Pharisees replied, "You are making those claims about yourself! Such testimony is not valid." ¹⁴ Jesus told them, "These claims are valid even though I make them about myself. For I know where I came from and where I am going, but you don't know this about me. ¹⁵ You judge me by human standards, but I do not judge anyone. ¹⁶ And if I did, my judgment would be correct in every respect because I am not alone. The Father[a] who sent me is with me. ¹⁷ Your own law says that if two people agree about

something, their witness is accepted as fact. **¹⁸** I am one witness, and my Father who sent me is the other."

¹⁹ "Where is your father?" they asked. Jesus answered, "Since you don't know who I am, you don't know who my Father is. If you knew me, you would also know my Father."**²⁰** Jesus made these statements while he was teaching in the section of the Temple known as the Treasury. But he was not arrested, because his time had not yet come.
²¹ Later Jesus said to them again, "I am going away. You will search for me but will die in your sin. You cannot come where I am going." **²²** The people[d] asked, "Is he planning to commit suicide? What does he mean, 'You cannot come where I am going'?"
²³ Jesus continued, "You are from below; I am from above. You belong to this world; I do not. **²⁴** That is why I said that you will die in your sins; for unless you believe that I AM who I claim to be, you will die in your sins."

²⁵ "Who are you?" they demanded. Jesus replied, "The one I have always claimed to be. **²⁶** I have much to say about you and much to condemn, but I won't. For I say only what I have heard from the one who sent me, and he is completely truthful." **²⁷** But they still didn't understand that he was talking about his Father. **²⁸** So Jesus said, "When you have lifted up the Son of Man on the cross, then you will understand that I AM he I do nothing on my own but say only what the Father taught me. **²⁹** And the one who sent me is with me—he has not deserted me. For I always do what pleases him."**³⁰** Then many who heard him say these things believed in him. **³¹** Jesus said to the people who believed in him, "You are truly my disciples if you remain faithful to my teachings. **³²** And you will know the truth, and the truth will set you free." **³³** "But we are descendants of Abraham," they said. "We have never been slaves to anyone. What do you mean, 'You will be set free'?"

³⁴ Jesus replied, "I tell you the truth, everyone who sins is a slave of sin. **³⁵** A slave is not a permanent member of the family, but a son is part of the family forever. **³⁶** So if the Son sets you free, you are truly free. **³⁷** Yes, I realize that you are descendants of

Abraham. And yet some of you are trying to kill me because there's no room in your hearts for my message. **38** I am telling you what I saw when I was with my Father. But you are following the advice of your father."

39 "Our father is Abraham!" they declared. "No," Jesus replied, "for if you were really the children of Abraham, you would follow his example. **40** Instead, you are trying to kill me because I told you the truth, which I heard from God. Abraham never did such a thing. **41** No, you are imitating your real father." They replied, "We aren't illegitimate children! God himself is our true Father."**42** Jesus told them, "If God were your Father, you would love me, because I have come to you from God. I am not here on my own, but he sent me….

48 The people retorted, "You Samaritan devil! Didn't we say all along that you were possessed by a demon?"**49** "No," Jesus said, "I have no demon in me. For I honor my Father—and you dishonor me. **50** And though I have no wish to glorify myself, God is going to glorify me. He is the true judge. **51** I tell you the truth, anyone who obeys my teaching will never die!" **52** The people said, "Now we know you are possessed by a demon. Even Abraham and the prophets died, but you say, 'Anyone who obeys my teaching will never die!' **53** Are you greater than our father Abraham? He died, and so did the prophets. Who do you think you are?"

54 Jesus answered, "If I want glory for myself, it doesn't count. But it is my Father who will glorify me. You say, 'He is our God,' **55** but you don't even know him. I know him. If I said otherwise, I would be as great a liar as you! But I do know him and obey him. **56** Your father Abraham rejoiced as he looked forward to my coming. He saw it and was glad."
57 The people said, "You aren't even fifty years old. How can you say you have seen Abraham?" **58** Jesus answered, "I tell you the truth, before Abraham was even born, I AM!" **59** At that point they picked up stones to throw at him. But Jesus was hidden from them and left the Temple." (NLT).

2. **Those who do not love and believe in Jesus Christ and his teachings are children of the devil (their Father, the "Murderer from the beginning...He is a liar & the Father of lies" vs 44) even if they are descendants of Abraham. They lack understanding, are spiritually blind, in spiritual slavery and therefore need salvation through Jesus Christ:**

John 8:43-47:
"⁴³ Why can't you understand what I am saying? It's because you can't even hear me! ⁴⁴ For you are the children of your father the devil, and you love to do the evil things he does. He was a murderer from the beginning. He has always hated the truth, because there is no truth in him. When he lies, it is consistent with his character; for he is a liar and the father of lies. ⁴⁵ So when I tell the truth, you just naturally don't believe me! ⁴⁶ Which of you can truthfully accuse me of sin? And since I am telling you the truth, why don't you believe me? ⁴⁷ Anyone who belongs to God listens gladly to the words of God. But you don't listen because you don't belong to God." (NLT).

Jesus Christ came into the world to fulfil the New Covenant promised to the descendants of Abraham, Isaac and Jacob and extended to the world through Christ.

Jesus' teachings highlighted and so affirmed that one's ethnicity as an Israelite, a descendant of Abraham does not guarantee one abundant life on earth or eternal life with Father God, because it does not automatically mean one is a legitimate child of Father God. Accepting and believing in Jesus Christ as the Messiah and as God in the flesh (2 Corinthians 5:19) regardless of ethnicity is the only means by which one is saved and therefore reconciled to Father God. A legitimate child of God is a true disciple of Jesus Christ.

Such a person is able to receive and also understand the Word of God planted in their hearts as promised in the New Covenant according to Jeremiah 31:31-34 (see Teaching at the end of this chapter) . This is because they are no longer spiritually blind or deaf, but have access to the revelatory realm of God, His wisdom, knowledge and understanding.

All are one in Christ

Abraham and his descendants were chosen by God as a nation through whom Jesus Christ came into the world as Saviour and Lord. God has promised that descendants of Abraham, Isaac and Jacob who have not yet accepted Jesus Christ as Lord and Saviour will be saved (Romans Chapters 10 & 11). They therefore also need to be evangelised by believers in Christ.

The Apostle Paul wrote to the Galatians (3:26-28) about how God relates to His children through Christ Jesus. Having been united with Christ, God sees and relates to each one of his children equally; He does not withhold anything from them (i.e. his blessings and love), nor treats them differently based on their nationality, ethnicity, social/economic class status or gender.

"[26] For you are all children of God through faith in Christ Jesus. [27] And all who have been united with Christ in baptism have put on Christ, like putting on new clothes. [28] There is no longer Jew or Gentile, slave or free, male and female. For you are all one in Christ Jesus." (Gal. 3:26-28 NLT).

PART 2

THE CHOSEN CHILDREN OF GOD AND THEIR ULTIMATE DESTINATION

I. **The disciples of Jesus Christ are the chosen among the called.**

1. **Being called does not mean one is chosen. To be chosen one has to demonstrate by confession and action that one accepts and believes in their heart that Jesus Christ is their Lord and Saviour.**

"For many are called, but few are chosen." (Matthew 22:14NLT).

2. **If one truly believes in Jesus, then it means one believes in the Father who alone draws people to Jesus.**

   i. The Father, the sovereign God of all is ultimately the one who decides who will be drawn to Jesus for the purpose of salvation.

   "For no one can come to me unless the Father who sent me draws them to me, and at the last day I will raise them up." (John 6:44NLT).

   -The Father knows the names of those who will
   - listen & learn from him or
   - allow Him, the vinedresser (John 15) to prune or purge them so that they bear more fruit.

   The names of these people are in the Lamb's book of life.

   Speaking of the New Jerusalem, the LORD said:

   "And all the nations will bring their glory and honor into the city. ^{27} Nothing evil will be allowed to enter, nor anyone who practices shameful idolatry and dishonesty—but only those whose names are written in the Lamb's Book of Life." (Rev.21:26-27 NLT).

   Father alone knows whose name is written in the Lamb's Book of Life. He draws them to Jesus Christ at specific times in their lives so that they would become children of God.

This is because according to God's plan, Jesus Christ is the only means to ensure that this predestined plan of their lives (to be children of God) comes to fruition.

God sent Jesus:
"For this is how God loved the world: He gave[a] his one and only Son, so that everyone who believes in him will not perish but have eternal life. (John 3:16NLT).

Jesus is the only way to the Father:
"6 Jesus told him, "I am the way, the truth, and the life. No one can come to the Father except through me. 7 If you had really known me, you would know who my Father is. From now on, you do know him and have seen him!" 8 Philip said, "Lord, show us the Father, and we will be satisfied."
9 Jesus replied, "Have I been with you all this time, Philip, and yet you still don't know who I am? Anyone who has seen me has seen the Father! So why are you asking me to show him to you? 10 Don't you believe that I am in the Father and the Father is in me? The words I speak are not my own, but my Father who lives in me does his work through me. 11 Just believe that I am in the Father and the Father is in me. Or at least believe because of the work you have seen me do." (John 14:6-11NLT).

ii. The Son, Jesus Christ receives and preserves those chosen by the Father to believe in him for it is the Son's mandate to do the will of the Father who sent him; as a reconciler of the Father and mankind.

"However, those the Father has given me will come to me, and I will never reject them." (John 6:37NLT).

Jesus' Ministry of Reconciliation:

At the end of Jesus' ministry his words confirm that he fulfilled the will of the Father, which was to receive all who Father sent to him (except Judas). This meant that they were reconciled to God through Jesus. They belonged to God which is why Jesus prayed as follows for them:

"Now I am departing from the world; they are staying in this world, but I am coming to you. Holy Father, you have given me your name; now protect them by the power of your name so that they will be united just as we are.[12] During my time here, I protected them by the power of the name you gave me. I guarded them so that not one was lost, except the one headed for destruction, as the Scriptures foretold.[13] "Now I am coming to you. I told them many things while I was with them in this world so they would be filled with my joy." (John 17:11-13NLT).

Believers in Jesus are likewise given a ministry of reconciliation:

"And God has given us this task of reconciling people to him. [19] For God was in Christ, reconciling the world to himself, no longer counting people's sins against them. And he gave us this wonderful message of reconciliation. [20] So we are Christ's ambassadors; God is making his appeal through us. We speak for Christ when we plead, "Come back to God!" [21] For God made Christ, who never sinned, to be the offering for our sin, so that we could be made right with God through Christ." (2 Corinthians 5:19NLT).

iii. Jesus' disciples are legitimate children of God because they not only know and accept Jesus, but they know and accept the God of Israel as well.

Jesus' disciples are those who abide by the terms of their relationship with him and these are also legitimate children of God. This is because those who know and accept Jesus, also know and accept the Father as well (John 8:19). They live according to his teachings or obey his commands. They are rewarded with Jesus' promises to his disciples which include

- having knowledge of the truth that sets free (John 8:31-32).
- living in the presence of God (John 14:23).

iv. Jesus' disciples, because of his love for them, have direct access to the Father to make personal requests in Jesus name. In addition there is an assurance of Father God's love and answered prayer.

"At that time you won't need to ask me for anything. I tell you the truth, you will ask the Father directly, and he will grant your request because you use my name. 24 You haven't done this before. Ask, using my name, and you will receive, and you will have abundant joy. 25 "I have spoken of these matters in figures of speech, but soon I will stop speaking figuratively and will tell you plainly all about the Father. 26 Then you will ask in my name. I'm not saying I will ask the Father on your behalf, 27 for the Father himself loves you dearly because you love me and believe that I came from God. 28 Yes, I came from the Father into the world, and now I will leave the world and return to the Father." (John 16:23-28 NLT).

II. Jesus' disciples are destined for eternal life in heaven with Jesus and Father God.

Jesus spoke in the same manner to his disciples as he did to the unbelieving Jews in general that where he was going they could not go, however while for one group (the unbelievers) it was a permanent prohibition for the other it was only a temporary one until God's appointed time for them to join him.

1. Message to those who were not believers in Jesus Christ: they are destined for hell unless they repent.

When speaking to the unbelieving Jews, Jesus basically told them that they could never go where he was going because they were destined to be with their father Satan as they were not his "sheep".

"He was in the Temple, walking through the section known as Solomon's Colonnade. [24] The people surrounded him and asked, "How long are you going to keep us in suspense? If you are the Messiah, tell us plainly."
[25] Jesus replied, "I have already told you, and you don't believe me. The proof is the work I do in my Father's name. [26] But you don't believe me because you are not my sheep." (John 10:23-26 NLT).

2. Message to those who are believers in Jesus: they are destined for heaven – Father God's dwelling.

Jesus gave a new commandment to his disciples and told them why they needed that commandment;
So now I am giving you a new commandment: Love each other. Just as I have loved you, you should love each other. [35] Your love for one another will prove to the world that you are my disciples."
[36] Simon Peter asked, "Lord, where are you going?" And Jesus replied, "You can't go with me now, but you will follow me later." (John 13:34-36 NLT).

Jesus assured his disciples that they will follow him afterwards when they were ready as they believed that he was from the Father. They were therefore destined to go where he was going which is to the Father. His purpose was to bring them to the Father where they will have eternal life (John 13:36).

Other scriptures of assurance to the disciples of Jesus' devotion to them and their ultimate destiny:

"Don't let your hearts be troubled. Trust in God, and trust also in me. ² There is more than enough room in my Father's home. If this were not so, would I have told you that I am going to prepare a place for you? ³ When everything is ready, I will come and get you, so that you will always be with me where I am. ⁴ And you know the way to where I am going."

⁵ "No, we don't know, Lord," Thomas said. "We have no idea where you are going, so how can we know the way?"

⁶ Jesus told him, "I am the way, the truth, and the life. No one can come to the Father except through me. ⁷ If you had really known me, you would know who my Father is From now on, you do know him and have seen him!"

⁸ Philip said, "Lord, show us the Father, and we will be satisfied."

⁹ Jesus replied, "Have I been with you all this time, Philip, and yet you still don't know who I am? Anyone who has seen me has seen the Father! So why are you asking me to show him to you? ¹⁰ Don't you believe that I am in the Father and the Father is in me? The words I speak are not my own, but my Father who lives in me does his work through me. ¹¹ Just believe that I am in the Father and the Father is in me. Or at least believe because of the work you have seen me do.

¹² "I tell you the truth, anyone who believes in me will do the same works I have done, and even greater works, because I am going to be with the Father. ¹³ You can ask for anything in my name, and I will do it, so that the Son can bring glory to the Father. ¹⁴ Yes, ask me for anything in my name, and I will do it!" (John 14:1-14 NLT).

¹⁶ "In a little while you won't see me anymore. But a little while after that, you will see me again."

¹⁷ Some of the disciples asked each other, "What does he mean when he says, 'In a little while you won't see me, but then you will see me,' and 'I am going to the Father'? ¹⁸ And what does he mean by 'a little while'? We don't understand."
¹⁹ Jesus realized they wanted to ask him about it, so he said, "Are you asking yourselves what I meant? I said in a little while you won't see me, but a little while after that you will see me again. ²⁰ I tell you the truth, you will weep and

mourn over what is going to happen to me, but the world will rejoice. You will grieve, but your grief will suddenly turn to wonderful joy. ²¹ It will be like a woman suffering the pains of labor. When her child is born, her anguish gives way to joy because she has brought a new baby into the world. ²² So you have sorrow now, but I will see you again; then you will rejoice, and no one can rob you of that joy." (John 16:16-22 NLT).

"²⁷ My sheep listen to my voice; I know them, and they follow me. ²⁸ I give them eternal life, and they will never perish. No one can snatch them away from me, ²⁹ for my Father has given them to me, and he is more powerful than anyone else. No one can snatch them from the Father's hand. ³⁰ The Father and I are one." (John 10:27-30 NLT).

Teaching ~ Encouragement

The New Covenant; Jesus, the Holy Spirit & Partakers of the New Covenant.

The New Covenant was first mentioned in the Old Testament in the Book of Jeremiah,

> "The day is coming," says the LORD, "when I will make a new covenant with the people of Israel and Judah. 32 This covenant will not be like the one I made with their ancestors when I took them by the hand and brought them out of the land of Egypt. They broke that covenant, though I loved them as a husband loves his wife," says the LORD. 33 "But this is the new covenant I will make with the people of Israel after those days," says the LORD. "I will put my instructions deep within them, and I will write them on their hearts. I will be

their God, and they will be my people. 34 And they will not need to teach their neighbors, nor will they need to teach their relatives, saying, 'You should know the LORD.' For everyone, from the least to the greatest, will know me already," says the LORD. "And I will forgive their wickedness, and I will never again remember their sins." (Jeremiah 31:31-34 NLT)

The Old Covenant God established with the Israelites required that they obey the Mosaic law. The law required the people to perform rituals and sacrifices to God for the forgiveness of their sins.

The New Covenant mentioned in Jeremiah 31:33 (also Hebrews 8:8-12) was fulfilled when Jesus Christ came to establish a new covenant between God and His people, Israel which was extended as prophesied in times of old and demonstrated in Jesus ministry to Gentiles (non-Israelites).

"When God speaks of a "new" covenant, it means he has made the first one obsolete. It is now out of date and will soon disappear." (Hebrews 8:13 NLT)

THE NEW COVENANT IS "WRITTEN" ON THE HEARTS OF CHRISTIANS

The Mosaic or Old Covenant (Hebrews 8:6, 13, 2 Corinthians 3:14) was written in stone and beneficial in that it enabled Israel to know what the righteousness of God entails and what sin was but without a permanent remedy of salvation from sin. However the New Covenant, which redeems both Israelites and Gentiles from being under the penalty of the law (condemnation due to sin) is "written on our hearts" and one can only partake of it through faith in Christ Jesus, whose crucifixion resulted in the shedding of his blood to make atonement for the sins of the world.

"So now there is no condemnation for those who belong to Christ Jesus. 2 And because you belong to him, the power of the life-giving Spirit has freed you[b] from the power of sin that leads to death. 3 The law of Moses was unable to save us because of the weakness of our sinful nature. So God did what the law could not do. He sent his own Son in a body like the bodies we sinners have. And in that body God declared an end to sin's control over us by giving his Son as a sacrifice for our sins." (Romans 8:1-3 NLT).

"25 In the same way, he took the cup of wine after supper, saying, "This cup is the new covenant between God and his people—an agreement confirmed with my blood. Do this to remember me as often as you drink it." (1 Corinthians 11:25 NLT)

"15 That is why he is the one who mediates a new covenant between God and people, so that all who are called can receive the eternal inheritance God has promised them. For Christ died to set them free from the penalty of the sins they had committed under that first covenant."(Hebrews 9:15 NLT)

"24 You have come to Jesus, the one who mediates the new covenant between God and people, and to the sprinkled blood, which speaks of forgiveness instead of crying out for vengeance like the blood of Abel." (Hebrews 12:24 NLT)

ANYONE CAN BE A CHILD OF GOD THROUGH ACCEPTANCE OF JESUS CHRIST AS LORD AND SAVIOUR AND THEREFORE PARTAKE OF THE NEW COVENANT.

Those who accept Christ as Lord and Saviour partake of the New Covenant because they accept his death, burial and resurrection as a means of deliverance from sin;

"8 In fact, it says, "The message is very close at hand; it is on your lips and in your heart." And that message is the very message about faith that we preach: 9 If you openly declare that Jesus is Lord and believe in your heart that God raised him from the dead, you will be saved. 10 For it is by believing in your heart that you are made right with God, and it is by openly declaring your faith that you are saved." (Romans 10:8-10 NLT).

As the New Covenant is partaken of by confession and faith in Jesus as Lord and Saviour, the believer is given a free gift of salvation; saved by grace through faith alone and not by works (Ephesians 2:8-9). Their salvation means they are reconciled to God through Jesus, the "seed of the Woman" (Genesis 3:15) who "crushed" the head of the serpent or came to destroy the works of the devil (1 John 3:8).

"For God in all his fullness was pleased to live in Christ,20 and through him God reconcile everything to himself. He made peace with everything in heaven and on earth by means of Christ's blood on the cross. 21 This includes you who were once far away from God. You were his enemies, separated from him by your evil thoughts and actions. (Colossians 1:19-21 NLT)"

"27 And all who have been united with Christ in baptism have put on Christ, like putting on new clothes. 28 There is no longer Jew or Gentile, slave or free, male and female. For you are all one in Christ Jesus. 29 And now that you belong to Christ, you are the true children of Abraham. You are his heirs, and God's promise to Abraham belongs to you." (Galatians 3:27-29 NLT).

HOW WILL MEN KNOW GOD OR HAVE HIS LAWS WRITTEN ON THEIR HEARTS (JEREMIAH 31:33-34)?

BY THE HOLY SPIRIT INDWELLING MAN'S HEART WHICH OCCURS DURING SALVATION WHEN ONE ACCEPTS JESUS AS PERSONAL SAVIOUR AND THEREFORE ENTERS INTO THE NEW COVENANT.

"He has enabled us to be ministers of his new covenant. This is a covenant not of written laws, but of the Spirit. The old written covenant ends in death; but under the new covenant, the Spirit gives life."(2 Corinthians 3:6 NLT).

We are "able ministers of the New Testament" or covenant by way of the Spirit, the Spirit of God which gives us life. Jesus is also "the Second Adam, the life-giving Spirit" (1 Corinthians 15:45). Jesus said as the Light of the world, he gives the "Light of Life" to those who come to him (Romans 8:12) and is their "Resurrection and Life" (John 11:25).

WHO IS THE HOLY SPIRIT TO THE BELIEVER AND IN RELATION TO GOD & JESUS?

The Holy Spirit is the Spirit of God and was sent by God at the request of Jesus. This is because Jesus knew he would no longer be physically present with his disciples, following his death, burial, resurrection and ascension to Father. He desired that anyone who believed in him would have the Holy Spirit, the Spirit of God dwelling in their hearts so that they will not be as orphans in his physical absence (John 14:16/Acts 1:8/Acts 2).

The Holy Spirit is the power of God indwelling the believer and endows them with the anointing or power of God to be Christ-like and therefore able to live a life in reconciliation with God (Col 1:20), thus in essence being restored to the image of God in which human beings were created by Him (Genesis 1:26-27).

The Holy Spirit, the Spirit of Truth, reminds the believer of the teachings of Jesus (John 14:26) and therefore testifies of him (John 15:26-27). The Holy Spirit is the Spirit of Prophecy; the testimony of Jesus (Rev 19:10), for Jesus embodies prophetic fulfilment. The Holy Spirit, who is the Spirit of God, knows His thoughts and reveals them to mankind (1 Corinthians Chapter 2:9-12).

Thus the function of the Holy Spirit, also known as Spirit of Truth who guides believers into all truth (John 16:13) is the same as that of Christ Jesus in that he enables reconciliation of mankind to God. The planting of God's word in one's heart (according to the promise of God in Jer. 31:31-34) therefore happens in this manner; A knowing of who Jesus and God are, is made possible by the Holy Spirit as the partaker of the New Covenant is constantly taught by the Holy Spirit according to the Word of God and reminded of the teachings of Jesus. Inevitably this means the Word or scriptural truths are understood by revelation for those who are in fellowship with the Holy Spirit.

In the last days, the true worshippers will worship God in Spirit and in His truth as according to John 4:24. The era following the ascension of Jesus and the day of Pentecost when the Holy Spirit was poured mightily upon numerous people of different nationalities and races was the era of commencement of the Apostolic Prophetic church of the last days. Therefore the term

'Last Days' is applied from that time and thereafter until the Second Coming of Jesus and Joel 2:28-32 (NLT) is being fulfilled:

"Then, after doing all those things, I will pour out my Spirit upon all people. Your sons and daughters will prophesy. Your old men will dream dreams, and your young men will see visions. 29 In those days I will pour out my Spirit even on servants—men and women alike. 30 And I will cause wonders in the heavens and on the earth—blood and fire and columns of smoke. 31 The sun will become dark, and the moon will turn blood red before that great and terrible day of the Lord arrives. 32 But everyone who calls on the name of the Lord will be saved, for some on Mount Zion in Jerusalem will escape, just as the Lord has said. These will be among the survivors whom the Lord has called." (Joel 2:28-32 NLT).

CHAPTER 7

WHAT'S IN A TITLE? DESCRIPTIONS OF THE MISSION OF JESUS' DISCIPLES

1. AMBASSADORS OF CHRIST

Their role as Ambassadors of Christ is through the church of which Christ Jesus is the head and comprises of the unity of believers within the spiritual Kingdom of God. This Kingdom is under the ruler-ship of Abba Father.

Jesus Christ, Head of the Church

"Christ is also the head of the church, which is his body. He is the beginning, supreme over all who rise from the dead. So he is first in everything." (Colossians 1:18NLT).

"So we are Christ's ambassadors; God is making his appeal through us. We speak for Christ when we plead, "Come back to God!"
(2 Corinthians 5:20NLT).

2. A KINGDOM OF PRIESTS

"... for you are a chosen people. You are royal priests, a holy nation, God's very own possession. As a result, you can show others the goodness of God, for he called you out of the darkness into his wonderful light". (1 Peter 2:9 NLT).

This is what the angels said of Jesus and what he did:
"You are worthy to take the scroll and break its seals and open it. For you were slaughtered, and your blood has ransomed people for God from every tribe and language and people and nation.[10] And you have caused

them to become a Kingdom of priests for our God. And they will reign on the earth."
(Rev 5:9-10).

3. MINISTERS OF RECONCILIATION

"[11] Because we understand our fearful responsibility to the Lord, we work hard to persuade others. God knows we are sincere, and I hope you know this, too. [12] Are we commending ourselves to you again? No, we are giving you a reason to be proud of us, so you can answer those who brag about having a spectacular ministry rather than having a sincere heart. [13] If it seems we are crazy, it is to bring glory to God. And if we are in our right minds, it is for your benefit. [14] Either way, Christ's love controls us. Since we believe that Christ died for all, we also believe that we have all died to our old life.

[15] He died for everyone so that those who receive his new life will no longer live for themselves. Instead, they will live for Christ, who died and was raised for them. So we have stopped evaluating others from a human point of view. At one time we thought of Christ merely from a human point of view. How differently we know him now! [17] This means that anyone who belongs to Christ has become a new person. The old life is gone; a new life has begun!

[18] And all of this is a gift from God, who brought us back to himself through Christ. And God has given us this task of reconciling people to him. [19] For God was in Christ, reconciling the world to himself, no longer counting people's sins against them. And he gave us this wonderful message of reconciliation. [20] So we are Christ's ambassadors; God is making his appeal through us. We speak for Christ when we plead, "Come back to God!" [21] For God made Christ, who never sinned, to be the offering for our sin, so that we could be made right with God through Christ. (2 Corinthians 5:11-21 NLT).

Reconciliation in this context means that a change in a life has made it possible for that life to be reconnected or reconciled with the one the life was originally connected with. This act of reconnection was made possible by the act of someone else. This act of reconciliation by Jesus in his death, burial and resurrection was for the purpose of reconciling mankind with Abba Father, man's creator and God.

When one lives a Christ-like life it means that he or she is "dead to self" or has overcome the desire to give in to carnal cravings and satanic temptations and through obedience to Christ's commands lives in God's presence (John 14:21,23/John 8:12,32).

When a believer in Jesus Christ is reconciled to God, it means that he or she is also given the Ministry of Reconciliation (as an Ambassador of Christ or among the Royal Priesthood/Holy Nation). The Ministry of Reconciliation in action encompasses fulfilling the commission to (Matthew 28:18-21/Mark 16:17-18):

- Preach,
- Evangelise,
- Disciple,
- Heal the sick /deliver the demon possessed and to
- Live a daily lifestyle as a witness of Abba Father to the unbelieving world.

4. "EPISTLE OF CHRIST"/"ABLE MINISTERS OF THE NEW TESTAMENT NOT OF THE LETTER, BUT OF THE SPIRIT".

Believers in Jesus are
- "a letter from Christ…This "letter" is written not with pen and ink, but with the Spirit of the living God. It is carved not on tablets of stone, but on human hearts." (2 Corinthians 3:3 NLT).

- "ministers of his new covenant. This is a covenant not of written laws, but of the Spirit. The old written covenant ends in death; but under the new covenant, the Spirit gives life." (2 Corinthians 3:6 NLT).

In context: "Are we beginning to praise ourselves again? Are we like others, who need to bring you letters of recommendation, or who ask you to write such letters on their behalf? Surely not!² The only letter of recommendation we need is you yourselves. Your lives are a letter written in our hearts; everyone can read it and recognize our good work among you. ³ Clearly, you are a letter from Christ showing the result of our ministry among you. This "letter" is written not with pen and ink, but with the Spirit of the living God. It is carved not on tablets of stone, but on human hearts.
⁴ We are confident of all this because of our great trust in God through Christ. ⁵ It is not that we think we are qualified to do anything on our own. Our qualification comes from God.⁶ He has enabled us to be ministers of his new covenant. This is a covenant not of written laws, but of the Spirit. The old written covenant ends in death; but under the new covenant, the Spirit gives life." (2 Corinthians 3:1-6 NLT)

What does "The old written covenant ends in death; but under the new covenant, the Spirit gives life." (verse 6) Mean?
The King James version of the bible puts it this way *"for the letter killeth, but the spirit giveth life."*

The Law of Moses had two aspects to it, the Ceremonial Laws and Moral Law (Ten commandments). The Ceremonial Laws were done away with for they were foreshadows or types of Christ. However the Moral Law (Ten Commandments) was not eradicated but perfected by Christ Jesus where this perfection was needed.

Therefore the meaning of "The letter kills but the Spirit gives life" is not that all the laws of ancient Israel (under the term "the Law of Moses") should be ignored or treated as not applicable but some are, and those that are (Ten commandments) are applicable because the Spirit of God through Christ Jesus, the "Last Adam and Life-giving Spirit" (1 Corinth. 15:45) has perfected them through his teaching which gives his followers knowledge and understanding as to how they should be interpreted according to the will of God. The teachings of Jesus in Matthew 5 to Chapter 7 are evidence of this.

If interpreted this way (in obedience), they will be spiritually revived. If not it would be as though they were merely 'the letter'; To explain this further, the letter in this sense (verse 6) means the Law of Moses in the Old Testament context, which was used by God for His purposes at the time, however in New Testament times if the law is not interpreted as Christ would have it, it is void of the life of God and therefore inducing spiritual death.

The Moral Law should therefore be obeyed in the context of the New Covenant (in the New Testament) of Christ. The New Covenant was a fulfilment of God's promise to Israel (Jeremiah 31:31-34) and extended to all who believe in Jesus Christ; God was saying that He would write His laws on human hearts (2 Corinth. 3, verse 3 connected with verse 6).

Furthermore, if you have natural knowledge of things (including the bible) and understanding from them derived from your own interpretation or that of mere men with worldly wisdom, this knowledge and understanding is merely of 'the letter that kills' category as they are void of the life of God. Having a zeal for and knowledge of scripture even to degree or doctorate level does not automatically result in God imparting Spiritual gifts such as supernatural knowledge, wisdom and understanding. Spiritual gifts are given by God to whom God chooses. He may choose an uneducated person over an educated person, even with degrees to impart Spiritual gifts. Why? This is because He is the Most High God (Creator, Sovereign and possessor of the whole world) and can make choices that do not necessarily appeal to people.

Jesus is the giver of the Holy Spirit "Living Waters" to believers in him. The Holy Spirit is the Life of God within Jesus' disciple. Therefore the Life of God within a believer in Christ makes it possible for them to interpret scripture as

revealed to them by the Spirit. This sustains spiritual empowerment and enables them to live a Christ-like life and to do great works for God.

"On the last day, the climax of the festival, Jesus stood and shouted to the crowds, "Anyone who is thirsty may come to me! [38] Anyone who believes in me may come and drink! For the Scriptures declare, 'Rivers of living water will flow from his heart."(John 7:37-38 NLT)

Jesus promised to quench the thirst of those who come to him (John 7:37-38). Anyone who believes in him will have flowing out of their heart "rivers of living water". Jesus was speaking about the fact that those who come to him will be saturated with the Holy Spirit (living water) to over flowing. As a result, they become instruments for the outflow of God's Spirit and works to the glory of His name. The Holy Spirit is one who those who believed in him were to receive following his resurrection and ascension as Jesus promised (John 14:26, Acts 2).

The appropriateness of such an invitation at the end of the Feast of the Tabernacles is noteworthy as it came after the discourse between Jesus and the Jews at the Feast of tabernacles, a discourse which exposed the spiritual blindness (hence a dryness –lack of "living waters") of the unbelieving Jews. Jesus was offering a spiritual awakening to all present at the Feast as to who he and God are. At the Feast of Tabernacles, Jesus' invitation (John 7:37-38NLT) is expressing just one of the many blessings the disciples receive from him who is the fulfilment the New Covenant. This blessing is the impartation of The Holy Spirit from whom the believer in Jesus receives revelatory gifts so that one can receive among other things, healing from spiritual blindness and so be able to "see" and therefore know God through Jesus.

The Feast of Tabernacles celebrates when God made his abode with His people in the wilderness and sheltered them as they journeyed from Egypt through the wilderness until they arrived in Canaan, the land God gave them. God will abide with anyone who accepts Jesus Christ as their Lord and Saviour as He did with Israel in the wilderness.

Deliverance from spiritual blindness is by way of The Holy Spirit who knows the mind of God and imparts His wisdom (1 Corinthians 2) to those in fellowship with God through Jesus Christ. The Holy Spirit also teaches, testifies of Jesus Christ and reminds Jesus' disciples of his teachings (John 14:26/15:26-27). Jesus personifies the Word of God:

In the beginning the Word already existed.
   The Word was with God,
   and the Word was God.
² He existed in the beginning with God.
³ God created everything through him,
   and nothing was created except through him.
⁴ The Word gave life to everything that was created,
   and his life brought light to everyone.
⁵ The light shines in the darkness,
   and the darkness can never extinguish it.
⁶ God sent a man, John the Baptist, ⁷ to tell about the light so that everyone might believe because of his testimony. ⁸ John himself was not the light; he was simply a witness to tell about the light. ⁹ The one who is the true light, who gives light to everyone, was coming into the world. ¹⁰ He came into the very world he created, but the world didn't recognize him. ¹¹ He came to his own people, and even they rejected him. ¹² But to all who believed him and accepted him, he gave the right to become children of God. ¹³ They are reborn—not with a physical birth resulting from human passion or plan, but a birth that comes from God.
¹⁴ So the Word became human and made his home among us. He was full of unfailing love and faithfulness. And we have seen his glory, the glory of the Father's one and only Son." (John 14:1-14 NLT).

5. CARER OF EARTH: THE ADAMIC MANDATE TO TEND TO THE LAND (EARTH) IS RESTORED TO EVERY BELIEVER IN CHRIST.

The fulfilment of Jesus' ministry on earth, his death, burial, resurrection and ascension back to the Father was a mediation which brought about reconciliation of man with their creator, Father God.
This is confirmed in the following scriptures: "For there is only one God and one Mediator who can reconcile God and humanity-- the man Christ Jesus." (1Timothy 2:5NLT).

"**14** Just think how much more the blood of Christ will purify our consciences from sinful deeds so that we can worship the living God. For by the power of the eternal Spirit, Christ offered himself to God as a perfect sacrifice for our sins. **15** That is why he is the one who mediates a new covenant between God and people, so that all who are called can receive the eternal inheritance God has promised them. For Christ died to set them free from the penalty of the sins they had committed under that first covenant. (Hebrews 9:14-15 NLT).

God so loved the world He created that He came in the person of Jesus Christ to redeem it, so as to restore it back to himself (2 Corinthians 5:19/John 3:16).

i. The redemption of the world, everything in it, starts with the redemption of man.

Man's salvation is through confession and belief in his heart that Jesus Christ is Lord and Saviour.

"**9** If you openly declare that Jesus is Lord and believe in your heart that God raised him from the dead, you will be saved. **10** For it is by believing in your heart that you are made right with God, and it is by openly declaring your faith that you are saved." (Romans 10:9-10 NLT).

After man is saved or reconciled to God, it means that he has direct access to God through Jesus Christ, or by praying directly to Father, but in Jesus' name:

²³ At that time you won't need to ask me for anything. I tell you the truth, you will ask the Father directly, and he will grant your request because you use my name. ²⁴ You haven't done this before. Ask, using my name, and you will receive, and you will have abundant joy.

²⁵ "I have spoken of these matters in figures of speech, but soon I will stop speaking figuratively and will tell you plainly all about the Father.²⁶ Then you will ask in my name. I'm not saying I will ask the Father on your behalf, ²⁷ for the Father himself loves you dearly because you love me and believe that I came from God. (John 16:23-27NLT)

ii. Man was originally called in service to God for the sake of the environment or creation (animals, plant life etc...) on planet earth.

Scriptural insights as to the fact that mankind has been given the role by God to tend to the earth and creation in general are as follows:

- God gave Adam dominion over the earth and told him to subdue it (Gen 1:28), this was part of Adam and his descendants' God given blessing as was the command to be "fruitful and multiply" or to be productive in every way.

  "²⁸ Then God blessed them and said, "Be fruitful and multiply. Fill the earth and govern it. Reign over the fish in the sea, the birds in the sky, and all the animals that scurry along the ground." (Gen 1:28 NLT).

Mankind was granted the authority to "govern" or "reign" on earth over all living creatures. God was giving human beings the ability, authority and power to do as they liked on planet earth. While human beings have free will, they were created in the image of God and the entrustment to dominate and rule by God is therefore intended to be a blessing. Therefore the expectation is that human beings will do all they have been instructed to do according to the will of God. In other words they will take care of the environment and other living things to the glory of God.

- God placed Adam in the garden to tend to it (Genesis 2:15) and

- God entrusted the naming of all the livestock to Adam after he created him.
  (Genesis 2:20).

iii. The born again Christian's mandate is to continue Christ's work of reconciling the world back to God.

"[19] For all creation is waiting eagerly for that future day when God will reveal who his children really are. [20] Against its will, all creation was subjected to God's curse. But with eager hope, [21] the creation looks forward to the day when it will join God's children in glorious freedom from death and decay." (Romans 8:19-21 NLT).

As God came in person to restore the world back to himself in the person of Christ, he depends on those who come to Him through Christ to continue Christ's mission of world reconciliation back to God. This is a daily calling of the children of God

The Christian's mission through Christ is to be understood as beyond living a committed relationship with God and bringing human beings to salvation. In other words they have a responsibility which is far beyond being in

1) Relationship with God and others as according to God's commands.

36 "Teacher, which is the most important commandment in the law of Moses?" 37 Jesus replied, "'You must love the Lord your God with all your heart, all your soul, and all your mind.' 38 This is the first and greatest commandment. 39 A second is equally important: 'Love your neighbor as yourself.' 40 The entire law and all the demands of the prophets are based on these two commandments." (Matthew 22:36-40 NLT).

2) Service to God for the sake of mankind as expressed in

Matthew 28:18-21: "[18] Jesus came and told his disciples, "I have been given all authority in heaven and on earth. [19] Therefore, go and make disciples of all the nations, baptizing them in the name of the Father and the Son and the Holy Spirit. [20] Teach these new disciples to obey all the commands I have given you. And be sure of this: I am with you always, even to the end of the age."(NLT).

Mark 16:15-18: "[15] And then he told them, "Go into all the world and preach the Good News to everyone. [16] Anyone who believes and is baptized will be saved. But anyone who refuses to believe will be condemned. [17] These miraculous signs will accompany those who believe: They will cast out demons in my name, and they will speak in new languages. [18] They will be able to handle snakes with safety, and if they drink anything poisonous, it won't hurt them. They will be able to place their hands on the sick, and they will be healed." (NLT).

When one becomes a child of God or a disciple of Jesus, it is important for them to understand that their mission includes service to God for the sake of creation in addition to mankind, this is because they continue the "reconciliation of the world back to God" process began by Christ Jesus. As the apostle Paul said, creation is awaiting eagerly the manifestation of the children of God; it is awaiting the rising up of God's people as according to their calling after they are saved, so that "[21] the creation looks forward to the day when it will join God's children in glorious freedom from death and decay." (Romans 8:21NLT).

It is when a person is aligned to the will of God through the born again experience that he is able to fulfil God's mandate for him in terms of caring for the world at large as according to the will of God. The Christian is empowered to do so because he or she has access to God and His Spiritual power and gifts.

Teaching ~ Encouragement

Taking Stock: What Kind of a Disciple are You?

In Luke 9:57-62 we read about three potential disciples of Jesus. Brethren as we enter into the New Year, it is important to take stock of this year and the previous years that we have walked with the LORD.

This account of three potential disciples is one of many biblical accounts which will help us. It will enable us to think things through, confess our sins and repent and decide to be more vigilant if we need to, as well as give God thanks for what He has done and is about to do.

I. Potential Disciple no. 1

"And it came to pass, that, as they went in the way, a certain [man] said unto him, Lord, I will follow thee whithersoever thou goest.58And Jesus said unto him, Foxes have holes, and birds of the air [have] nests; but the Son of man hath not where to lay [his] head." (Luke 9:57-58 KJV).

This man decided to follow Jesus by himself. Jesus' reply implies that he was asking the man whether he had considered the cost of following him. Jesus at the time did not have his own accommodation. It is noteworthy that Jesus did not tell him what to do but gave his own life as an example of the type of life the man would have if he follows Jesus.
If you have chosen to follow God, you must know that you have covenanted to be Christ-like and so should be ready to pay the price.

Jesus was saying "Have you counted the cost?", "can you pay the price of homelessness or going from place to place and so not being guaranteed accommodation or a comfortable life?"

What has your Christian life been like until this point? Are you aware of the costs or do you count the cost of following Jesus Christ?

Morris Cerullo in the devotional "Journey into the promised Land" lists some of the costs of following Christ as follows
1. Sacrifice as well as service (1 John 3:16)
2. Loneliness (2 Timothy 1:15)
3. Rejection and criticism (John 1:11)
4. Persecution (2 Corinthians 11:23-27).

It is only those who live in the reality that there are indeed costs and have made a conscious decision to not only consider them daily but are willing to go through them, who are able to live victorious Christian lives.

II. Potential Disciple no. 2

" 59And he said unto another, Follow me. But he said, Lord, suffer me first to go and bury my father.60Jesus said unto him, Let the dead bury their dead: but go thou and preach the kingdom of God." (Luke 9:59-60 KJV).

When Jesus called this man, the man felt he could still continue making his own decisions and so prioritise his own desires I.e burying his father, as he had done before he was called. However Jesus' response is clear; the calling of God requires one to prioritise the kingdom of God or whatever God has called one to do as opposed to what one wants to do.

Please know that Jesus was not saying one's parents or family are not important or that we should not attend to them. Nothing must be placed before the call of God. Jesus loved his family a sign being when on the cross of crucifixion, he spoke in a manner to both his mother and John that gave John the Apostle the understanding that Jesus wanted him to take care for his mother, so John took her into his home after Jesus died (John 19:25-27).

This was also revealed when Jesus spoke to the people and someone told him is mother and brethren wanted to speak to him. He replied
"48… Who is my mother? and who are my brethren?
"49And he stretched forth his hand toward his disciples, and said, Behold my mother and my brethren! 50For whosoever shall do the will of my Father which is in heaven, the same is my brother, and sister, and mother." (Matt.12:48-50 KJV)

As we can see, as with the first potential disciple, Jesus was teaching his "do as I do" principle for despite his love for his family, Jesus prioritised the work of the ministry over and above them which was the will of God.

Brethren, do you prioritise your will over and above that of the will of God?

Your response maybe "well I often don't know God's will so I just get on with what I want to do and hope it is".
If this is the case, my prayer is that you would spend time in fasting and prayer even as you enter into 2016 asking the Lord to reveal His will for your life to you and also that you would refrain from making hasty decisions and learn to wait on the Lord.

III. Potential Disciple no. 3

"61And another also said, Lord, I will follow thee; but let me first go bid them farewell, which are at home at my house.62And Jesus said unto him, No man, having put his hand to the plough, and looking back, is fit for the kingdom of God." (Luke 9:61-62 KJV). This man wanted to follow the Lord, however he wanted to take time to do something first, or wanted to follow God but on his own terms. Jesus' reply affirms the motives of the man's heart; He was holding onto his past life, torn between committing to God wholeheartedly and living in the world.

Brethren, as you may know, when God calls us, he requires us to respond immediately and not to start thinking of what we have left undone and need to do first, or put off obeying God until it suits us. At times we may decide to do something first which we convince ourselves is part of or compliments the calling of God or what He is asking us to do. Partial obedience is not obedience.

I pray to God that everyone reading this will from henceforth be more sensitive to God's leading in your lives so that you will not hesitate to know what He is calling you to do. Also that God would grant you an increased measure of His gift of discerning of spirits and the ability to stay in the place of praise, prayer, bible reading and meditation. This is so that as you abide in this realm consistently, you will be able to hear God's voice in whichever way He chooses to speak to you. In Jesus name Amen.

CHAPTER 8

JESUS AND HIS ENEMIES, THE UNBELIEVING JEWS

PART 1
Jesus Defies His Enemies

The consequences of the unbelieving Jews not knowing Father (God) - they could not receive or accept the Son nor his works.

Introduction
Jesus came to Perfect the Law of Moses not to do away with it. What constituted the Law of
Moses in Old Testament times?
The Law of Moses constitutes a list of Moral laws (which includes the Ten Commandments), rituals/ceremonial laws (sacrifices, offering) and guidance (i.e. food, purity) which God gave to Moses (Malachi 4:4). This is why they are named after him. They can be found in the Old Testament books of Exodus, Leviticus, Numbers and Deuteronomy. The Hebrew Israelites were instructed to abide by the Law of Moses (Deut.4:1).

What was the purpose of the Law of Moses?
From the New Testament we read that the Law of Moses was for the purpose of teaching the children of Israel. It also enabled them to know right from wrong or what sin was (Gal.3:17,19, 22-23).

JESUS THE PERFECTER OF THE LAW
Jesus said "Don't misunderstand why I have come. I did not come

to abolish the Law of Moses or the writings of the prophets, No, I came to accomplish their purpose". The King James version of the bible replaces accomplish with fulfil (Matthew 5:17 NTL).

1. **The Jewish religious leaders – their rigid pursuit to fulfil the law of Sabbath keeping, prevented them from accepting & so rejoicing in God at work through Jesus Christ.**

HEALING OF THE LAME MAN ON THE SABBATH

The man who had been an invalid for 38 years was told by the religious leaders that he was forbidden to carry his mat on the Sabbath (John 5:1-14).

The Religious Leaders were disinterested in the works of God (in this case healing) when these works were not done within their approved days. They were greatly offended when

- the healing was done on the Sabbath
- the one healed carried his mat on the Sabbath

Why? The healing and carrying of the mat were considered works and should not be undertaken on the Sabbath. Doing so on the Sabbath violated the Law of Moses as interpreted by the religious leaders.

It is noteworthy that after he explained that the man who made him well told him to pick up his mat and walk, the Jews did not utter words of praise to God that the man had been healed they just asked who healed him. The fact that Jesus was healing was not celebrated, instead when and how he healed was criticised by the religious leaders who demanded everything be done according to the Law of Moses.

There was a disinterest in the fact that an infirmed human being had been healed regardless of the day of the healing. They were offended that the man who was healed was doing something they considered "work" in this case carrying his mat, which was forbidden on the Sabbath day.

Why did Jesus heal on the Sabbath? Jesus' ways as those of God the Father are not man's ways; When and how Jesus healed a person was irrelevant, what was relevant was the fact that the person was healed. As in the time of Jesus' ministry, this is still God's principle. Those who place more importance on the method, the "when and how" something is done than on the fact that the anointing of God has resulted in the glorious end product i.e. healing, peace, salvation and wholeness, are missing the point and they do not know or understand the God of our Lord Jesus Christ.

Clearly God's ways are not man's ways:
"My thoughts are nothing like your thoughts," says the Lord. "And my ways are far beyond anything you could imagine." (Isaiah 55:8 NLT).

God is the creator and possessor of the whole universe (El Elyon) and He does as He pleases. The works of Abba Father through Jesus Christ are not restricted to a certain time or period or dependant on man's preferences. Jesus testifies of a Father who is constantly working and he does the same;
"16 So the Jewish leaders began harassing[a] Jesus for breaking the Sabbath rules. 17 But Jesus replied, "My Father is always working, and so am I." 18 So the Jewish leaders tried all the harder to find a way to kill him. For he not only broke the Sabbath, he called God his Father, thereby making himself equal with God" (John 5:16-18 NLT)

2. **The religious leaders accepted circumcision on the Sabbath but not that a man should be made whole; this represents judging by the letter (what was required by law) not by the Spirit.**

"14 Then, midway through the festival, Jesus went up to the Temple and began to teach. 15 The people were surprised when they heard him. "How does he know so much when he hasn't been trained?" they asked.16 So Jesus told them, "My message is not my own; it comes from God who sent me. 17 Anyone who wants to do the will of God will know whether my teaching is from God or is merely my own. 18 Those who speak for themselves want glory only for themselves, but a person who seeks to honor the one who sent him speaks truth, not lies. 19 Moses gave you the law, but none of you obeys it! In fact, you are trying to kill me."

20 The crowd replied, "You're demon possessed! Who's trying to kill you?"
21 Jesus replied, "I did one miracle on the Sabbath, and you were amazed. 22 But you work on the Sabbath, too, when you obey Moses' law of circumcision. (Actually, this tradition of circumcision began with the patriarchs, long before the Law of Moses.) 23 For if the correct time for circumcising your son falls on the Sabbath, you go ahead and do it so as not to break the law of Moses. So why should you be angry with me for healing a man on the Sabbath? 24 Look beneath the surface so you can judge correctly." (John 7:14-24 NLT)

Righteous judgement vs judgement by "mere appearance"

Why did Jesus accuse the Jews of judging by mere appearance (John 7:24) when they chose to reject healing on the Sabbath but accepted circumcision on the Sabbath? This is because they were basing their resistance on the 'dos and don'ts' of the Mosaic law or what was perceived as right or wrong based on their interpretation of the Mosaic Law. The act of circumcision was a commandment by God and therefore had been traditionally accepted as an undertaking even on the Sabbath. They did not however class healing by Jesus (who they did not believe was from God) and its outcome (i.e. a healed man, holding his mat) as acceptable on the Sabbath. *What was classed as "work" was prohibited even if it was an act resulting in the wellbeing of mankind such as healing.* Jesus taught that there should be right judgement used in deciding whether something should be done on the Sabbath or not. How could they classify the healing of a man on the Sabbath as inferior to circumcision? That was not righteous judgement.

As far as Jesus was concerned the unbelieving Jews were wrongfully interpreting the Law of Moses. They accepted circumcision on the Sabbath, but not the healing of a human being. This reveals their lack of compassion for the infirmed as well as their attempts to find reasons to condemn and accuse Jesus. In addition, this focus on rigid adherence to the law regardless of the problems it caused reveals not only their lack of compassion, but also how spiritually blind and deaf the unbelieving Jews were.

As a result, they were prevented from accepting and partaking of God's supernatural works through Jesus Christ, the Messiah who is also the Life Giving Spirit "…The Scriptures tell us, "The first man, Adam, became a living person. "But the last Adam—that is, Christ—is a life-giving Spirit." (1 Corinthians 15:45 NLT).

The promise of abundant life in the present world & eternal life was prohibited in the lives of the unbelieving Jews because it had not been received.

I. JESUS A COMPASSIONATE SAVIOUR WAS BOLD IN THE FACE OF OPPOSITION.

1. **Jesus Christ is a compassionate Saviour who cares for the physical & emotional condition of mankind and intervenes regardless of laws, even those instructed by God.**

Jesus was and is still interested in the physical and emotional condition of human beings for he came to set the captives of Satan free (Isaiah 61) whether they are bound by sin or sickness.

It is clear that the paralysed condition of the man in John 5 was as a result of his life of sin for following his healing Jesus said to him:

"…Now you are well; so stop sinning, or something even worse may happen to you." (John 5:14 NLT).

When the healed man found out it was Jesus who had healed him after he saw Jesus again, he told the Jews and "So the Jewish leaders began harassing Jesus for breaking the Sabbath rules." (John 5:16 NLT).

2. Jesus Christ was bold in the face of opposition.

The unbelieving Jews including religious leaders criticised Jesus several times, one of those times was when he healed the paralysed man on the Sabbath (John 5). Jesus' ministry was founded on doing the will of God and therefore not for the purpose of pleasing others. As a result he was not concerned that he angered the unbelieving Jews to the point that they tried to kill him.

As well as being criticised for healing on the Sabbath, Jesus was criticised because he spent time in the company of tax-collectors and sinners (Matthew 9:10). This did not bother him, he said to his enemies "Now go and learn the meaning of this Scripture: "I want you to show mercy, not offer sacrifices." For I have come to call not those who think they are righteous, but those who know they are sinners." (Matthew 9:13NLT).

In addition, even though Jesus knew that he would be criticised for speaking to a woman (John 4) with an immoral lifestyle who was a Samaritan (a people considered unapproachable and inferior by the Israelites), this did not stop Jesus from approaching her and ministering to her. These examples confirm that Jesus was bold or fearless in what he did and how he did it. His boldness was because

-He knew the Father was with him because he was doing His will.

-He was focused on his God given mission and consumed with compassion for the masses and the zeal of fulfilling his mission.

In Jesus' ministry, he was testifying of himself as the Christ, one who is anointed. He had the anointing of the Spirit of the 'Sovereign Lord' (Isaiah 61:1) to set the captives of Satan free. The Spirit of God empowers and imparts boldness or fearlessness in the face of opposition so that one is able to fulfil the will of God. Jesus Christ is exemplary because he was anointed with the Holy Spirit who is the power of God and as a result was extremely efficient in his role as Saviour, deliverer and healer.

"And you know that God anointed Jesus of Nazareth with the Holy Spirit and with power. Then Jesus went around doing good and healing all who were oppressed by the devil, for God was with him."(Acts 10:38 NLT).

PART 2

The unbelieving Jews and Religious Leaders: lacked knowledge of the Son (Jesus), so could not know the Father (God).

Introduction

Jesus spoke of the unbelieving Jews who included religious leaders, as those who were blind yet they thought they could see (John 9:39-41). In other words they lacked knowledge and understanding, or if they had the knowledge, they lacked understanding about who God the Father was and of Old Testament accounts which point to Jesus Christ being the Messiah. The unbelieving Jews' reaction to Jesus' healing on the Sabbath was because of their Spiritual blindness to the fact that Jesus Christ was God incarnate or God in the flesh and it exposed their lack of knowledge of God and his nature as a compassionate Father to mankind. This nature of love in action is affirmed by God is one that must be the pursuit of all believers in Jesus Christ and should be demonstrated by them at all costs even if it makes them unpopular and open to criticism and opposition as in the case of Jesus Christ.

A Psalm that reveals mankind's worth to God:

Psalm 8
O LORD, our Lord, your majestic name fills the earth!
    Your glory is higher than the heavens.
² You have taught children and infants
    to tell of your strength,
silencing your enemies
    and all who oppose you.
³ When I look at the night sky and see the work of your fingers—
    the moon and the stars you set in place—
⁴ what are mere mortals that you should think about them,
    human beings that you should care for them?
⁵ Yet you made them only a little lower than God
    and crowned them with glory and honor.
⁶ You gave them charge of everything you made,
    putting all things under their authority—
⁷ the flocks and the herds
    and all the wild animals,
⁸ the birds in the sky, the fish in the sea,
    and everything that swims the ocean currents.
⁹ O LORD, our Lord, your majestic name fills the earth! (NLT).

1. The unbelieving Jews thought they knew Jesus Christ, Abba Father and Moses but they did not.

i. Jesus and Abba Father

JESUS SAID THEY DID NOT KNOW HIM NOR THE FATHER. IF THEY KNEW THE FATHER THEN THEY WOULD KNOW HIM.

Jesus said they did not know the Father because they (John 5:36-45)

1. did not believe Jesus' works on behalf of the Father which in themselves bore witness to Jesus,
2. did not believe the fact that Father Himself bore witness to Jesus,
3. have neither heard God's voice at any time, nor seen his shape,
4. do not have God's Word abiding in them,
5. do not have God's love in them.

Some Jews in Jerusalem thought they knew Jesus and where he was from and therefore concluded that he could not be the Messiah, because they felt that when the Christ comes no one will know where he is from (John 7:25-27).

Jesus replied (John 7:28-29) by agreeing with them that they knew where he was from and who he was in the natural sense (i.e. family, lineage and birth place) however they did not know the one who sent him (Abba Father) while he, Jesus did. Jesus and the Father are one (John 10:30).

Jesus is the "Way" (John 14:6) to his Father and so if they do not know him as the true Messiah, then they have no access to his Father who is the God they say they worship. As far as Jesus was concerned (John 14:7-11), anyone who sees, believes in him or his works and is in relationship with him has seen and believes in the Father God. The "Jesus" the unbelieving Jews and religious leaders thought they knew, was one of their own making, a mere human being who was not the Son of God or from God despite the evidence from their scriptures. However, the true Jesus Christ who is one with Father God was unknown by them.

ii. Moses.

THEY DID NOT REALLY BELIEVE MOSES, IF THEY DID THEN

THEY WOULD BELIEVE WHAT JESUS SAID BECAUSE MOSES WROTE ABOUT HIM.

Jesus again exposed the spiritual blindness of the unbelieving Jews by saying that they did not believe Moses because

"If you really believed Moses, you would believe me, because he wrote about me. **47** But since you don't believe what he wrote, how will you believe what I say?" (John 5:46-47 NLT)

2. Some of Jesus' disciples ceased from believing in him because they were offended by his words which they did not understand.

When Jesus preached that he was the bread of life and said that eternal life is only obtainable if his flesh was eaten and his blood was drunk, many were offended by his words and ceased from following him.

"Many of his disciples said, "This is very hard to understand. How can anyone accept it?"
61 Jesus was aware that his disciples were complaining, so he said to them, "Does this offend you? **62** Then what will you think if you see the Son of Man ascend to heaven again? **63** The Spirit alone gives eternal life. Human effort accomplishes nothing. And the very words I have spoken to you are spirit and life. **64** But some of you do not believe me." (For Jesus knew from the beginning which ones didn't believe, and he knew who would betray him.) **65** Then he said, "That is why I said that people can't come to me unless the Father gives them to me."
66 At this point many of his disciples turned away and deserted him. (John 6:60-66 NLT).

They took what he said literally and so did not understand this manner of speaking because they were spiritually blind as to who Jesus was. Jesus was merely vocalising what was going to happen to him; His death, burial and resurrection which people partake of (i.e. eating his body and drinking his blood) when they accept him as their Lord and Saviour by confession and belief in him (Romans 10:9-10).

This means they receive eternal life as well as a current life of abundant life through forgiveness of sins, healing from infirmities and other blessings rooted in the covenant of God to his people, Israel and the church.

"The thief's purpose is to steal and kill and destroy. My purpose is to give them a rich and satisfying life." (John 10:10 NLT).

3. Some of the Jews could not believe in Jesus because they lacked understanding when Jesus taught i.e. on where he was going.

"But Jesus told them, "I will be with you only a little longer. Then I will return to the one who sent me. 34 You will search for me but not find me. And you cannot go where I am going."35 The Jewish leaders were puzzled by this statement. "Where is he planning to go?" they asked. "Is he thinking of leaving the country and going to the Jews in other lands?[a] Maybe he will even teach the Greeks! 36 What does he mean when he says, 'You will search for me but not find me,' and 'You cannot go where I am going'?" (John 7:33-36 NLT).

4. Some of the unbelieving Jews including religious leaders chose to believe a lie about Jesus' city of origin.

"When the Temple guards returned without having arrested Jesus, the leading priests and Pharisees demanded, "Why didn't you bring him in?" [46] "We have never heard anyone speak like this!" the guards responded. [47] "Have you been led astray, too?" the

Pharisees mocked. ⁴⁸ "Is there a single one of us rulers or Pharisees who believes in him? ⁴⁹ This foolish crowd follows him, but they are ignorant of the law. God's curse is on them!" ⁵⁰ Then Nicodemus, the leader who had met with Jesus earlier, spoke up. ⁵¹ "Is it legal to convict a man before he is given a hearing?" he asked. ⁵² They replied, "Are you from Galilee, too? Search the Scriptures and see for yourself—no prophet ever comes from Galilee! (John 7:45-52 NLT).

There were some in Jerusalem who expressed doubt as to who Jesus was. This was when they spoke about knowing him and where he is from, thinking that if he was the true Messiah then no one will know where he is from (John 7:27). In addition while some people believed in him because of what he said, others expressed doubt by saying

"Others said, "He is the Messiah." Still others said, "But he can't be! Will the Messiah come from Galilee? 42 For the Scriptures clearly state that the Messiah will be born of the royal line of David, in Bethlehem, the village where King David was born."(John 7:41-42 NLT)

What springs to mind is this "surely if they took time to search the scriptures and compare the prophecies about this Jesus before them as well as his place of birth and lineage they would know that he was the Messiah!" The reason for assuming that Jesus Christ was a Galilean was either merely due to the fact that research was not undertaken to find out the truth of his origin or it was a deliberate ploy to spread the lie that he was a Galilean so as to discredit him. Considering the religious leaders were the most educated men of their day, who were among those who said he was a Galilean, it can be concluded that it was a collective deliberate ploy on their part to discredit Jesus by saying he could not be the Messiah because he was a Galilean.

Counsel ~ Encouragement

How not to be an enemy of Jesus Christ

- Obeying and doing God's will should take precedence over obeying and acting upon any rules and regulations from ancient to present times that are contrary to the word of God and prevent compassionate action (as required by God) or the duty of care towards one's fellow human being.

- You are called to fulfil your God given mission on earth by demonstrating Christ-like zeal for the call of God and his compassion towards humanity regardless of where you are, what day of the week it is or who you are ministering to in terms of their ethnicity, race or gender. Someone's healing (as the paralysed man in John 5) and destiny (as the Samaritan woman in John 4) depends on your obedience and that person may not necessarily be of your ethnicity, race or gender. God may send them any time or day of the week, so it is important to be ready and available.

- As Jesus Christ, always remain focused on your God given mission however unconventional it might seem to some. Some people will always find reasons why you should not do something a certain way or they may frown at your strategy or idea. As long as you know God is leading you, is all that matters. Therefore be bold and fearless in the face of opposition. In your moments of weakness, as long as you abide in God, He will cause situations to work in your favour, strengthen and revive you by His Holy Spirit.

1. Love in Action is God in Action, for God is Love.

i. Compassion is love in action. Compassion was the foundation and "driving force" of Jesus' ministry.

The reason God sent Jesus Christ into the world was because of God's love for the world (John 3:16) and Jesus demonstrated this love in the way he ministered; by teaching and receiving converts into his kingdom, healing the sick and delivering the demon possessed.

Jesus showed compassion to the condemned and rejected. Compassion was the foundation and "driving force" of Jesus' ministry to the extent that he went against the status-quo and angered the unbelieving religious leaders. The life of a believer in Jesus Christ should be lived in like manner regardless of the danger of persecution by those who do not believe in Jesus Christ as Saviour and Lord. This is the essence of the New Covenant: "Love in Action" which means "God in Action" for "God is Love" (1 John 4:8 NLT)

ii. Love others with the love of God, even your enemies.

- **Love others**
  "[34] So now I am giving you a new commandment: Love each other. Just as I have loved you, you should love each other." (John 13:34NLT).

  Treat people as you would like to be treated.
  Matthew's gospel gives further insight into the commands of Jesus
  "Do to others whatever you would like them to do to

you. This is the essence of all that is taught in the law and the prophets." (Matthew 7:12NLT).

- **Love all, even your enemies.**
  [43] "You have heard the law that says, 'Love your neighbor' and hate your enemy. [44] But I say, love your enemies! Pray for those who persecute you! [45] In that way, you will be acting as true children of your Father in heaven. For he gives his sunlight to both the evil and the good, and he sends rain on the just and the unjust alike." (Matthew 5:43-45 NLT).

CHAPTER 9

THE BOND OF LOVE I – JESUS CHRIST AND HIS FEMALE SUPPORTERS

I. MARY OF BETHANY

Introduction

Mary or "Mary of Bethany" of John 11, Martha and Lazarus' sister is the same Mary mentioned by the disciples Matthew, Mark, Luke and John who anointed Jesus' head (Matthew 26:7/Mark 14:3) and feet (John 12 1-8, Luke 7:36-50). While the accounts in Matthew, Mark and Luke do not mention her name, Luke chapter 7 states she is the woman who lived a sinful life in that town and John's account of the anointing of Jesus in John 12 identifies her as the same Mary of John 11 who lives in Bethany with her sister Martha and brother Lazarus.

All three anointing accounts of Matthew, Mark and John reveal that the anointing took place in Bethany, Luke does not mention the place. We find out in John 12 that Jesus went to a dinner held in his honour in Bethany, although the name of the owner of the house is not mentioned, we know from Matthew and Mark that it was Simon the Leper's house, Luke says it was a Pharisee named Simon. According to John 12, Lazarus who Jesus rose from the dead (John 11) was at Simon's home in Bethany with his sister Martha who was serving and Mary who used the anointing oil to wash Jesus feet. At Simon's home as when Jesus was in Martha's home (John 11/Luke 10:38-42) it is evident that Mary is focused on Jesus, rather than helping her sister.

MARY'S UNCONDITIONAL LOVE DEMONSTRATED

1. **Despite being a woman, Mary of Bethany was bold in demonstrating her devotion to Jesus and learning from him.**

"As Jesus and the disciples continued on their way to Jerusalem, they came to a certain village where a woman named Martha welcomed him into her home. **39** Her sister, Mary, sat at the Lord's feet, listening to what he taught.**40** But Martha was distracted by the big dinner she was preparing. She came to Jesus and said, "Lord, doesn't it seem unfair to you that my sister just sits here while I do all the work? Tell her to come and help me." **41** But the Lord said to her, "My dear Martha, you are worried and upset over all these details! **42** There is only one thing worth being concerned about. Mary has discovered it, and it will not be taken away from her." (Luke 10:38-42 NLT)

Jesus, a Rabbi went against tradition by allowing a woman to sit at his feet to learn from him.
Mary of Bethany was demonstrating her eagerness to learn from Jesus when she sat at his feet and was his disciple although she did not have the title "Jesus' disciple". In that era it was unusual for a woman to be accepted as a disciple by a teacher or Rabbi.

2. **Mary of Bethany was eager to openly express her love & gratitude to Jesus by showing him total reverence and worship by the act of washing his feet with expensive perfume.**

"Six days before the Passover celebration began, Jesus arrived in Bethany, the home of Lazarus—the man he had raised from the dead. 2 A dinner was prepared in Jesus' honor. Martha served, and Lazarus was among those who ate with him. 3 Then Mary took a twelve-ounce jar of expensive perfume made from essence of nard, and she anointed Jesus' feet with it, wiping his feet with her hair. The house was filled with the fragrance.

4 But Judas Iscariot, the disciple who would soon betray him, said, 5 "That perfume was worth a year's wages. It should have been sold and the money given to the poor."
6 Not that he cared for the poor—he was a thief, and since he was in charge of the disciples' money, he often stole some for himself. 7 Jesus replied, "Leave her alone. She did this in preparation for my burial. 8 You will always have the poor among you, but you will not always have me." (John 12:1-8 NLT).

(Jesus comments here are very similar to those in Mark and Matthew).

Mary's great love for Jesus revealed a heart that was full of tremendous gratitude for her salvation from a life of sin as revealed in Luke's account:

"36 One of the Pharisees asked Jesus to have dinner with him, so Jesus went to his home and sat down to eat. 37 When a certain immoral woman from that city heard he was eating there, she brought a beautiful alabaster jar filled with expensive perfume. 38 Then she knelt behind him at his feet, weeping. Her tears fell on his feet, and she wiped them off with her hair. Then she kept kissing his feet and putting perfume on them.

39 When the Pharisee who had invited him saw this, he said to himself, "If this man were a prophet, he would know what kind of woman is touching him. She's a sinner!" 40 Then Jesus answered his thoughts. "Simon," he said to the Pharisee, "I have something to say to you."
"Go ahead, Teacher," Simon replied. 41 Then Jesus told him this story: "A man loaned money to two people—500 pieces of silver to one and 50 pieces to the other. 42 But neither of them could repay him, so he kindly forgave them both, canceling their debts. Who do you suppose loved him more after that?" 43 Simon answered, "I suppose the one for whom he canceled the larger debt." "That's right," Jesus said.

44 Then he turned to the woman and said to Simon, "Look at this woman kneeling here. When I entered your home, you didn't offer

me water to wash the dust from my feet, but she has washed them with her tears and wiped them with her hair. **45** You didn't greet me with a kiss, but from the time I first came in, she has not stopped kissing my feet. **46** You neglected the courtesy of olive oil to anoint my head, but she has anointed my feet with rare perfume. **47** "I tell you, her sins—and they are many—have been forgiven, so she has shown me much love. But a person who is forgiven little shows only little love." **48** Then Jesus said to the woman, "Your sins are forgiven." **49** The men at the table said among themselves, "Who is this man, that he goes around forgiving sins?" **50** And Jesus said to the woman, "Your faith has saved you; go in peace." (Luke 7:36-50 NLT).

II. MARY MAGDALENE[1]

Mary Magdalene demonstrated her love for Jesus when she

- joined other women, Jesus' mother, her sister Mary, the wife of Clopas near Jesus cross (John 19:25).

- was the first to go to Jesus' tomb and found it empty and went to tell Simon Peter and John (John 20:1-3). Mark 16:9-11 adds that when she told those who had been with him as they mourned and wept that he was alive they did not believe her.

Mary Magdalene woke up early to go to Jesus' tomb on the morning of the first day of the week and did not anticipate his resurrection so she thought people had taken his dead body away. In the Gospel of Mark and Luke we gain further insight into Mary Magdalene. In Mark 16:9 and Luke 8:2, Jesus is said to have cast seven demons out of Mary Magdalene. Mary Magdalene as Mary of Bethany was extremely grateful for being delivered and forgiven by Christ Jesus.

Gratitude was what compelled Mary to be totally devoted to Jesus. Mary Magdalene genuinely believed in Jesus as one sent by the God of Israel and felt immense gratitude that she was one of the people he delivered from demon possession. Father God who knows the heart condition of every human being knew the extent of this woman's pursuit of the Messiah and her devotion to him so it was His deliberate act to reward her by choosing her as the first one to see Jesus when he resurrected. God chooses to reward all his children in different ways.

III. FAITHFUL WOMEN WHO SUPPORTED JESUS' MINISTRY WERE PART OF HIS ENTOURAGE.

What is not often taught or deemed important to highlight is the fact that there were a number of women who formed part of Christ Jesus' valuable entourage as he went about teaching, healing and casting out demons.

"…Jesus began a tour of the nearby towns and villages, preaching and announcing the Good News about the Kingdom of God. He took his twelve disciples with him, along with some women who had been cured of evil spirits and diseases. Among them were Mary Magdalene, from whom he had cast out seven demons; [3] Joanna, the wife of Chuza, Herod's business manager; Susanna; and many others who were contributing from their own resources to support Jesus and his disciples. (Luke 8:1-3 NLT).

These women as an act of worship and gratitude for Jesus' ministry of teaching, healing and deliverance assumed the voluntary role of taking charge of the upkeep of Jesus and his disciples as they travelled around by "giving of their substance".

Many of these women who supported and followed Jesus were also discipled by him as the twelve men who were recognised as Jesus' disciples, but in that era women were traditionally not allowed to be disciples of a Teacher of Rabbi which Jesus was. Jesus allowed women to learn from him as is evident in the case of Mary of Bethany and in his discourse with the Samaritan woman which involved some teaching (John 4:4-26). Jesus was revealing as always what the New Covenant fulfilment through him entailed;

anyone regardless of their gender or race has access to the Father through Christ.

CONCLUSION

Jesus went against the status quo during his ministry

The act of allowing a woman to sit at his feet and learn from him, as well as travel from place to place with an entourage of women was not what a Rabbi of Jesus' day did. He must have been criticized. We know from scripture that Jesus was criticized for spending time with those considered sinners or of ill-repute. Jesus' deliberately stopped to converse with a Samaritan woman (John 4:4-26) for the purpose of transforming her life which he did successfully, she is recorded as having evangelised her family and people and Jewish Historian also states that she became a missionary. This was despite the fact that Samaritans were a people despised by the Israelites and considered inferior to them.

All the aforementioned confirms that Jesus' ministry went against the status quo and affirms that in terms of someone's relationship with Christ Jesus their gender, race, nationality or social status does not make them more or less worthy than another to merit his favour, teaching and most of all His love. God through Christ may choose to favour, heal or bless someone most people will ignore because of their gender, race, nationality or social status.

[1]Note: Mary Magdalene: some say she is the same person as Mary of Bethany. I have not had a revelation about that nor do I see any biblical scriptures to prove this and as a result I write about them separately.

Teaching ~ Encouragement

Loving Jesus

Jesus calls his disciples to be as Mary of Bethany – willing to pay a price for his sake regardless of criticism or persecution.

Jesus' words in response to Martha's (Luke 10:42) and Judas Iscariot's (John 12:4-8) complaints against Mary's actions should be understood as a message to his disciples in our day as then. Combining both responses by Jesus and knowing who he is, the message we receive from him is as follows:

"You will always have time to do your household chores or go about your everyday business and you will always have the poor among you, but the only thing you need, the one most important thing which will give you abundant and eternal life is to live a devoted, worshipful life unto me. Your willingness to pay a price, however heavy, to follow me or learn from me regardless of criticism or persecution will reveal the extent of your love for me."

A SECOND CHANCE MERITS EXPRESSIONS OF LOVE

There is a saying that goes like this "If at first you don't succeed try, try again!" Not many popular secular idioms or proverbs can be expressed in a Christian context but this one certainly can because rather than feel condemned and give up when we appear to fail, God's will is that we should trust him by depending on and partnering with him. This is what His "try again" means.

What we did not succeed in may not have been God's will in the first place anyway or the timing was not right and we were just trying to help God along to accelerate something we really wanted. As this was in our own strength it did not work out.

God is a God of second chances. When we confess our sins, He is faithful and just to forgive us and cleanse us from all unrighteousness (1 John 1:9). This is because our God is in the business of rebuilding damaged lives. Through the Prophet Jeremiah after telling Israel how much He loved her as a nation he went on to say "will build you up again and you will be rebuilt, O Virgin Israel. Again you will take up your tambourines and go out to dance with the joyful" (Jer.31:4).

Likewise God took us, new covenant believers from the kingdom of darkness to His kingdom through Jesus for the purpose of restoring to us once and for all the fellowship with God that humanity lost when Adam and Eve sinned.

Mary Magdalene

Mary Magdalene's expression of love to Jesus testifies to us that she had come to understand the depth of "everlasting (Jer. 31:3) love God had for her to the point of casting out seven demons from her (Luke 8:2/Mark 16:9) through Christ.

Mary Magdalene had been given a second chance in life, her sins had been blotted out to be remembered no more and she knew that she was no longer condemned because she lived for God through Christ Jesus (Romans 8:1-3).

Mary Magdalene expressed her heartfelt gratitude for her salvation by living for God through Christ Jesus. It was effortless because she loved Jesus and had made a conscious decision to live abiding in Him. Here are some of the examples of how she did so:

1.She was among the women who travelled to different towns or villages with Jesus and his disciples tending to their upkeep or financial needs (Luke 8:1-3). I would say that although she and the other women who were often with Jesus were not classed as "disciples of Jesus" as the twelve men were, they were also Jesus' disciples if we understand the definition of the word "disciple".

2.Mary Magdalene (see "note" at the end) is specified by name to have been a witness to three key events, the
a.**Crucifixion:** Mark 15:40, John 19:25, Matt. 27:56.
b.**Burial:** Mark 15:47, Matthew 27:61
Also brought spices with two other women to anoint Jesus' body (Mark 16:1).
c.**Resurrection – discovering the tomb was empty:**

Mark, Matthew and Luke indicate that Mary Magdalene was among the women who saw the empty tomb. John (20:1) mentions her as being the first to discover the tomb empty. The longer ending of the last chapter of Mark's gospel (sometimes left out) mentions that Jesus appeared to her first on her own following his resurrection.

Mary of Bethany

Mary of Bethany (see "note" at the end) is another woman who with Mary Magdalene and other women were often with Jesus and met his needs. Her utter devotion to Jesus was expressed in the Gospels as follows:

1.She chose the best thing to do as stated by Jesus when she preferred to sit at Jesus' feet and listen to his discourse instead of help her sister make preparations, presumably food.(Luke 10:38-42).

2. Mary of Bethany anointed Jesus with expensive perfumed oil and wiped his feet with her hair. John is the only account that identifies this Mary as the one who is sister to Martha and Lazarus (John 12:3 & John 11:1-2 are connected and the mention of Martha, suggest this Mary is the one of Luke 10:38-42).

Mary of Bethany had reason to devote her life to Jesus the way she did, savouring his every word and providing for him with the other women and using expensive oil on his feet. This is because she had been saved from a sinful life and was well known as such. This is evident in the Apostle Luke's account of the anointing of Jesus in which he says that she was a sinner (7: 36-37)

Her actions were touching: "And stood at his feet behind him weeping, and began to wash his feet with tears, and did wipe them with the hairs of her head, and kissed his feet, and anointed them with the ointment". (Luke 7:38 KJV)

Jesus describes that the reason why she loved so much was because she had been forgiven many sins. He added that her demonstration of faith had saved her (Luke 7:47). In the accounts of the Apostles Matthew (26:6-13) and Mark (14:3-9) regarding the anointing of Jesus' feet, the following was said by Jesus to show the immense blessings Mary of Bethany would receive for what she had done "I tell you the truth, wherever this gospel is preached throughout the world, what she has done will also be told, in memory of her". This is a principle of God; He honours those who honour Him (1 Sam 2:30 NIV).

It is highlighted in Luke 8:1-3 that the women who travelled with Jesus and his "recognized" disciples who were all male from place to place were ones "…who had been cured of evil spirits and diseases: Mary (called Magdalene) from whom seven demons had come out—and many others.." Society at the time did not consider women as disciples or ones to be instructed in the way men were. Their place of subordination in society was accepted.

Yet God considered women and particularly women who had infirmed and ungodly backgrounds prior to abiding in Christ, worthy to sit at his feet or follow him as disciples and be the first to see the empty tomb or receive the angelic visitation and announcement that Jesus had risen. Jesus often went against the status quo to make the point that God's ways are higher than that of man (Is 55:8-9) as well as only spiritually discerned by those who abide in Him through the Spirit (1 Corinthians 2).

God will always make a way for us to find God, abide in Him and serve Him and reap of the fruits for doing so regardless of our past lifestyle or our gender, race and social/economic class status.

In Jesus' time, being possessed by seven demons would have make one wonder of Mary Magdalene "what on earth was she involved in to have been in such a state!" and Mary of Bethany's past life of prostitution would have also caused eye brows to have been raised. However their testimony of deliverance should have highlighted to onlookers then as it should to us the kind of God we serve. He will not be more favourable with the one whose sin is defined as less serious in the eyes of man. To God sin is sin.

Having understood this, we ought to desire to each have the immense heart of gratitude Mary Magdalene (delivered from demon possession) and Mary of Bethany (delivered from a well known reputation as sinful, possibly prostitution) had regardless of how we or society have rated our sins. In other words, we are to see every type of sin as a great obstacle between us and God and so being forgiven our sins (whatever they may be and how many) is a major act of deliverance by God's mighty "hand" through Jesus' death burial and resurrection. This transition from the kingdom of darkness or Satan to that of God should be seen as the greatest escape of our lives and this is no exaggeration!

Thus in viewing our sins and deliverance in this manner inevitably puts us on a par with Mary Magdalene and Mary of Bethany for as they did, we instantly see the immense privilege we have as chosen to be children of God living under His grace and mercy while enjoying His provision, guidance and protection. We are therefore more likely to respond in total devotion as these women did.

A totally surrendered life is one that is greatly aware and impacted by the depth of love God has for us to the point that He sent his only begotten son, Jesus Christ to suffer death for us. Let us examine ourselves today, brothers and sisters; does our confession equate our devotion? By our fruits people will know whether we are truly His.

"For this cause I bow my knees unto the Father of our Lord Jesus Christ,[15] Of whom the whole family in heaven and earth is named,[16] That he would grant you, according to the riches of his glory, to be strengthened with might by his Spirit in the inner man;[17] That Christ may dwell in your hearts by faith; that ye, being rooted and grounded in love,[18] May be able to comprehend with all saints what is the breadth, and length, and depth, and height;[19] And to know the love of Christ, which passeth knowledge, that ye might be filled with all the fulness of God.[20] Now unto him that is able to do exceeding abundantly above all that we ask or think, according to the power that worketh in us,[21] Unto him be glory in the church by Christ Jesus throughout all ages, world without end. Amen.
(Eph.3:14-21 KJV).

<u>Note:</u> There is no scriptural evidence to support the fact that Mary Magdalene was a prostitute or the same person as Mary of Bethany although this was a popular belief in medieval western Christianity and some denominations or church groups today. From researching scriptures, confirmed by discernment, I conclude that they are two different women. I don't believe in facts that are not founded on scriptural accounts.

CHAPTER 10

THE BOND OF LOVE II - JESUS CHRIST, GOD THE FATHER AND THE DISCIPLES

I. THE LOVE RELATIONSHIP BETWEEN JESUS CHRIST AND FATHER GOD AND HOW THIS RELATIONSHIP IMPACTS ON THE WORLD.

A. How can one abide in the Father's love (which is also Jesus' love)?

1. The power of salvation through Jesus Christ – it enables his disciples to abide in the Father's love.

It was this same love for the world which compelled god to come into the world through Jesus Christ.

Jesus' love for his disciples is the same love with which the Father loved him. This type of love is an unconditional and sacrificial love. Jesus' disciples are called to abide within the realm of this type of love and in so doing they demonstrate it in every area of their lives. This is how the world will know that they are truly children of God.

"I have loved you even as the Father has loved me. Remain in my love." (John 15:9 NLT).

It is this same type of love that the Father demonstrated towards the world when He came in the person of Jesus to redeem it.

JESUS' ACCEPTANCE TO DIE ON THE CROSS WAS OUT OF OBEDIENCE TO THE FATHER BECAUSE HE LOVES THE FATHER, AND IS ONE WITH HIM.

Jesus obeyed the Father: "I don't have much more time to talk to you, because the ruler of this world approaches. He has no power over me,[31] but I will do what the Father requires of me, so that the world will know that I love the Father. Come, let's be going."(John 14:30-31 NLT)

Oneness with the Father: Jesus is not only the way to Father for humanity (John 14:6) through his death, burial and resurrection he is also one with Father for he said to Philip

"Anyone who has seen me has seen the Father. How can you say, 'Show us the Father'?" (John 14:9 NLT). Jesus also said "The Father and I are one." (John 10:30 NLT).

2. The power of obedience to Jesus who died a sacrificial death for world redemption (out of obedience to the father) – it enables his disciples to abide in the Father's love.

The ability to abide in Jesus' love (receive his love and live one's life rooted in his love) and therefore Father's love is made possible if we obey Jesus' commandments just as he kept the Father's commandments and abides in His love (John 15:10). Jesus always showed his disciples that his lifestyle was their example as to how to live their lives as God's children. It is therefore true to say that obedience to the Son (Jesus) and as a result being able to abide in his love, is as if one is obeying the Father. This is another way we are made to understand that Jesus is indeed the only means (John 14:6-7) to have access to God who is both creator and the God of Israel.

II. THE RELATIONSHIP BETWEEN JESUS AND HIS DISCIPLES IS A REVELATION OF GOD'S LOVE IN MANIFESTATION.

A. Abiding in the Father's love through obedience to Jesus

Christ.

1. What happens when the disciple abides in the Father's love through Jesus Christ?

Receiving Jesus' or the Father's love means one is secure in God and able to live a life rooted and grounded in true Godliness. As a result one is able to demonstrate God's unconditional and sacrificial love in their interpersonal relationship with others. The disciple of Jesus therefore becomes a true witness and a vessel through whom God loves the world.

2. What is the reward to the disciple who abides in the Father's love?

i. The Father and Jesus Christ are consistently present in their lives.

When one obeys Christ, it demonstrates one's love for him and results in intimacy with the Father in the power of the Holy Spirit.

Keeping Jesus' commandments demonstrates that his disciples love him and this will result in Father loving them and being consistently present in their lives.

"21 Those who accept my commandments and obey them are the ones who love me. And because they love me, my Father will love them. And I will love them and reveal myself to each of them." 22 Judas (not Judas Iscariot, but the other disciple with that name) said to him, "Lord, why are you going to reveal yourself only to us and not to the world at large?" 23 Jesus replied, "All who love me will do what I say. My Father will love them, and we will come and make our home with each of them. 24 Anyone who doesn't love me will not obey me. And remember, my words are not my own. What I am telling you is from the Father who sent me. 25 I am telling you these things now while I am still with you. 26 But when the Father sends the Advocate as my representative—that is, the Holy Spirit—he will teach you everything and will remind you of everything I have told you." (John 14:21-26 NLT).

PARENTING IN DEMONSTRATION

Thus obedience to Jesus is demonstration of one's love for him.

This reaps intimacy with the Father through Jesus which manifests as the presence of God in one's life; The Holy Spirit who Jesus prayed to the Father that He sends testifies of Jesus or bears witness to the fact that God and Jesus are present in the believer's life.

"For his Spirit joins with our spirit to affirm that we are God's children." (Romans 8:16 NLT)

"Then I fell down at his feet to worship him, but he said, "No, don't worship me. I am a servant of God, just like you and your brothers and sisters who testify about their faith in Jesus. Worship only God. For the essence of prophecy is to give a clear witness for Jesus." (Rev. 19:10 NLT).

The purpose for Jesus requesting for the Holy Spirit on behalf of believers is so that believers do not feel like orphans in the physical absence of Jesus.

"[26] But when the Father sends the Advocate as my representative—that is, the Holy Spirit—he will teach you everything and will remind you of everything I have told you. [27] "I am leaving you with a gift—peace of mind and heart. And the peace I give is a gift the world cannot give. So don't be troubled or afraid. [28] Remember what I told you: I am going away, but I will come back to you again. If you really loved me, you would be happy that I am going to the Father, who is greater than I am." (John 14:26-28 NLT).

The power of the Holy Spirit is at work to help the believer (who lives an obedient life unto God) in Jesus to live a fruitful life. This is a revelation of parenting by God through Jesus to bring the believer to a place of maturity so that they are effective in fulfilling their mandate as God's labourers and ambassadors on earth to the glory of God.

ii. In God's presence (intimate loving relationship, the result of obedience) is fullness of joy.

The receiving of Jesus' love, which is the Father's love through a lifestyle of obedience to Jesus means that one leads a life in the presence of the Father. Having just given counsel that in order to live in his love the disciple must obey his commandments, Jesus then said "I have told you these things so that you will be filled with my joy. Yes, your joy will overflow!" (John 15:11 NLT).

"You will show me the way of life, granting me the joy of your presence and the pleasures of living with you forever" (Psalm 16:11 NLT).

iii. There is a graduation from servanthood to intimate friendship if Jesus' disciples obey his commandments. As a friend, a disciple has access to communication with the Father.

"You are my friends if you do what I command. I no longer call you slaves, because a master doesn't confide in his slaves. Now you are my friends, since I have told you everything the Father told me. You didn't choose me. I chose you. I appointed you to go and produce lasting fruit, so that the Father will give you whatever you ask for, using my name. This is my command: Love each other." (John 15:14-17 NLT)

IN SUMMARY:

    Obedience:
- makes a way for the presence or glory and joy of God to manifest in one's life.

- gives the status of intimate friend of God and Jesus, and so one is able to communicate with the Father and empowered to overcome any demonic affliction and resistance to the fulfilment of one's prophetic identity and destiny.

B. AS A MASTER, JESUS DEMONSTRATED HIS SERVANT OR HUMBLE HEART;

AN UNCONDITIONAL AND SACRIFICIAL LOVE TOWARDS HIS DISCIPLES WHEN JESUS

i. washed their feet.

This demonstrates that

1. Jesus loves his own (disciples) in the world until the end;
   Before the Passover festival, Jesus knew that the time had come for him to leave this world and go back to the Father. Jesus loved his own who were in the world, and he loved them to the end. (John 13:1).
   This included Judas (whose feet Jesus washed as well) who was called of God to be among the disciples only for the purpose of his mandate as a betrayer of Jesus Christ (John 13:2, 18).

   His disciples belong to him:
   "When Jesus came to Simon Peter, Peter said to him, "Lord, are you going to wash my feet?" 7 Jesus replied, "You don't understand now what I am doing, but someday you will."8 "No," Peter protested, "you will never ever wash my feet!" Jesus replied, "Unless I wash you, you won't belong to me." (John 13:6-8 NLT).

2. By this act of washing of their feet, the disciples were declared washed all over not just their feet (John 13:10) meaning that they were declared sanctified, holy or set apart unto God through Christ.

3. If the master can stoop and wash his subordinates' feet, thus humbling himself, so they too can wash each

other's feet. For this was an example to them that they should do to each other as he had done to them.

"After washing their feet, he put on his robe again and sat down and asked, "Do you understand what I was doing? [13] You call me 'Teacher' and 'Lord,' and you are right, because that's what I am. [14] And since I, your Lord and Teacher, have washed your feet, you ought to wash each other's feet. [15] I have given you an example to follow. Do as I have done to you." (John 13:12-15 NLT).

This was a literal commandment as well as a means to teach that

- brethren in Christ and
- leaders in Christian service

must be willing to demonstrate their unconditional and sacrificial love for one another by accepting to be servants in humble service to one another as he had done by washing his disciple's feet.

There was to be a greater revelation of his humility, unconditional and sacrificial love for the world when he "stooped low" and died on the cross even though he was their "Master".

Though he was God, he did not think of equality with God as something to cling to. 7 Instead, he gave up his divine privileges[b]; he took the humble position of a slave and was born as a human being, When he appeared in human form, 8 he humbled himself in obedience to God and died a criminal's death on a cross. (Phil 2: 6-8 NLT)

JESUS CAME TO LOVE AND SERVE THOSE WHO

ARE HIS - BEING CHRISTLIKE IS HAVING THE SAME SENSE OF OBLIGATION TOWARDS OTHERS AS CHRIST DID.

As in the case of Jesus their master, the authority and power bestowed upon the disciples of Jesus to enable them to be effective in a Christlikeness manner is in no way threatened or diminished because of their show of humility and love in interpersonal relationships (John 13:13-16).

ii. died a sacrificial death on the Cross.

Jesus told them to love one another as he, their master loved them. He called his disciples friends and not servants and was willing to die on their behalf. "This is my commandment: Love each other in the same way I have loved you. There is no greater love than to lay down one's life for one's friend." (John 15:12-13 NLT)

The kind of love with which Jesus loved his disciples is affirmed as sacrificial because it is the greatest love one can show their friend. This is the kind of love which compelled Jesus to accept death for the sake of his friends.

Jesus commanded his disciples or friends to love one another with this same kind of selfless, sacrificial and unconditional love.

Teaching ~ Encouragement

Loving God and others

1. Obedience to God and Christ means we love them:
"If you love me, obey my commandments." (John 14:15 NLT)

Two Greatest Commandments:
"Teacher, which is the most important commandment in the Law of Moses?"
37 Jesus replied, "'you must love the Lord your God with all your heart, all your soul, and all your mind.' 38 This is the first and greatest commandment. 39 A second is equally important: 'Love your neighbour as yourself.' 40 The entire law and all the demands of the prophets are based on these two commandments." (Matthew 22:36-40 NLT)

- When you love God and demonstrate His unconditional love towards others and you accept that you have a duty of care towards them by virtue of being a child of God, then it means that you are in essence doing what you are fundamentally required to do as God's child through Christ.

- When you live a life as a believer in Jesus Christ, you are called to demonstrate the will of God which inevitably reveals his unconditional love.

2. The "1-2-3 Domino Effect" of the two Greatest Commandments and the Power of Forgiveness

"How we see ourselves, how we conduct our interpersonal

relationships are fruitful unto God, only if our relationship with God is according to His commands" **D.E. Nyamekye.**

36Master, which [is] the great commandment in the law?37Jesus said unto him, Thou shalt love the Lord thy God with all thy heart, and with all thy soul, and with all thy mind.38This is the first and great commandment.39And the second [is] like unto it, Thou shalt love thy neighbour as thyself.40On these two commandments hang all the law and the prophets." (Matthew 22:36-40 KJV)

THE 1-2-3 DOMINO EFFECT OF THE TWO GREATEST COMMANDMENTS

Point 1 – Point 2 – Point 3 Domino Effect

Let us ensure that the two greatest commandments are always at the forefront of our minds so that we

POINT 1 – Sustain a love relationship with God through a worshipful life (bible study, praise, prayer..) which includes focus on God in all that we do and do them as unto Him.

This is the only way we can

POINT 2 – Love ourselves because it is in this place that we learn to love ourselves by understanding who we are in God and who He is to us.

As a result of Point 2 out worked from Point 1 of the 1-2-3 Domino Effect, (whatever position we hold in the Body of Christ or society – in God's eyes a servant's heart is the mark of an obedient heart – Jesus is our example)
We are able to

POINT 3 – Love our neighbours (anyone: friend, spouse, colleague, acquaintance etc…); this means we are able to demonstrate God's love through us to others meaning

– we are able to have compassion for people

– empathise with them
– care about their feelings so as to be cautious how we treat them, ensuring we are not doing or saying anything to hurt them nor lording over them …
-treat others as we would like to be treated.

Prayer: Father, help us in our weakness so that we live according to these two greatest commandments. Thank you for answering this prayer in my life and that of my brethren. In Jesus' mighty name I pray Amen

THE POWER OF FORGIVENESS
Satan exerts himself in his attempt to ruin interpersonal relationships in general and especially those between Christian friends, spouses, ministers, work colleagues and acquaintances, because he is a sly crafty, cunning fool who will do anything to attempt to bring chaos in the harmony that is the 1-2-3 Domino Effect of the Two Greatest commandments.

Let us take heed not to let the hurts inflicted upon us from childhood through to adulthood or what people are doing currently to hurt or upset us (it may not even be deliberate) prevent us from having or sustaining the peace we have in the knowledge that we are lovable or significant human beings created in the image of God and restored as such through Christ for His pleasure and purposes. The born again experience opens the door for us to be healed from lies Satan has said about who we are and our worth especially through others. Our healing starts with forgiving all those who have hurt us directly or indirectly and contributed to these lies about our identity and worth.

Forgiveness by God and therefore making peace with Him is conditional to our forgiving others. This is why Jesus included these words in the prayer he taught his disciples to pray *^{12} And forgive us our debts, as we forgive our debtors. (Matthew 6:14-15 KJV)*
There is an assumption therefore that his disciples know that they should forgive their debtors so that God will forgive them.

After this, he emphasised the point by saying:"¹⁴ *For if ye forgive men their trespasses, your heavenly Father will also forgive you:* ¹⁵ *But if ye forgive not men their trespasses, neither will your Father forgive your trespasses."* (Matthew 6:14-15 KJV).

When we forgive, we receive forgiveness from father which means cleansing from all unrighteousness and so a way is made for us to have fellowship with God through the Holy Spirit. Un-forgiveness is a decision not to demonstrate the love of God to our "neighbour" (Point 3), it is therefore disobedience and as sin, disobedience also separates us from God and so we are prevented from loving God with all our heart, mind and soul (Point 1). Without loving God, we cannot love ourselves or sustain the unconditional God kind of love (Point 2).

Forgiveness is the key to overcoming Satan's attempts at creating discord, causing contention and hatred between Christians so that they do not demonstrate the love of God for one another (Point 3 of the 1-2-3 Domino Effect). This is often because when people are hurt, they are likely to fall into temptation as they are angry, discouraged, disappointed and begin to exercise thoughts of retaliation which range from either not speaking to the one who has hurt them or doing something to hurt them as well.

The importance of forgiveness is reinforced by Jesus, expressing the heart of God on the matter when he said that
-you must forgive those who have sinned against you not 7 times but 70 x 7 times (Matthew 18:21-22); In other words forgiveness should be a perpetual lifestyle attitude of a children of God.
-when you are bringing your offering to God and you remember that someone has something against you then you must first go and reconcile with them before doing so. (Matthew 5:23-24)

God also cares about that person who has something against you whether they are Christians or not and so should you, is what Jesus is saying. Your "neighbour" (Matthew 22) is not necessarily a fellow Christian and approaching them to make peace means you desire to obey God's command that you love your neighbour. Your neighbour could also be your enemy, in relation to this Jesus taught as follows:

You have heard the law that says, 'Love your neighbor' and hate your enemy. [44] *But I say, love your enemies! Pray for those who persecute you!* [45] *In that way, you will be acting as true children of your Father in heaven. For he gives his sunlight to both the evil and the good, and he sends rain on the just and the unjust alike.* [46] *If you love only those who love you, what reward is there for that? Even corrupt tax collectors do that much. (Matthew 5:43-46 NLT)*

It is evident therefore that the responsibility to cultivate harmonious co-existence (hence expressing the love of God) lies with the disciple of Jesus and forgiveness is the key. When used therefore, this key not only opens the door to a sustained relationship of love with God but it also serves to keep us within the realm of the 1-2-3 Domino Effect (Two Greatest Commandments) cycle all the days of our lives.

To God be the glory great things He has done!

ABOUT THE AUTHOR

In addition to being a Writer, Poet and Published Author, Deborah Esther Nyamekye is a Prophetess, Intercessor, Teacher/Trainer and Entrepreneur. Her mandate is to be a prophetic voice, teacher and writer to the Glory of God; encouraging, counselling, teaching and training people to know and fulfil their God given destinies and to live holy lives according to the will of the God of our Lord and Saviour Jesus Christ. Deborah is also an advocate and prophetic voice in the area of inter-racial relations and social justice.

Deborah has served the Body of Christ in several areas over the years, these include evangelism, discipleship, cell group and intercessory prayer leadership as well as being part of healing and prophetic ministry teams.

Deborah felt the call of the LORD to start Bearwitness-Forerunner Ministries International in 2013. It comprises of Ready Writer Prophetic Scribe Ministry and Maranatha Encounter Ministry. Ready Writer Prophetic Scribe Ministry is a channel for Deborah's prolific writing ministry (e.g. inspirational teachings, prophetic exhortations, poetry, prayers, songs/psalms…). Its outlets include book publication (Light of the World-John8.12 publishing), "Manna from on High" blog (www.readywriterps451.org), Online Magazines, one being Nice Column by Shira (www.nicecolumnbyshira.com) and the use of some social media.

Maranatha Encounter Ministry is the outlet through which Deborah organises teaching/training and prophetic gatherings and partners with other ministries' events. It is also the platform through which Deborah receives prayer and prophecy requests via webmail.

For more information:
Bearwitness-Forerunner Ministries International
Website: https://bearwitness-forerunner.org
Twitter: https://twitter.com/bw_forerunner
Email: admin@bearwitness-forerunner.org
Amazon Author Page: https://amazon.com/author/nyamekyede

©March 2016 Light of the World-John8.12 Publishing
All rights reserved.
ISBN 978-0-9931738-5-1

Made in the USA
Columbia, SC
20 May 2017